From An Ec

A practical guide to c

by **Suzanne Ruthven**
Editor of Quartos Magazine

ignotus

ignotus press
BCM-Writer, London WC1N 3XX

British Library Cataloguing in Publication Data
(to be applied for)
ISBN: 0 9522689 1 4

Cover design: Jim Riley

Cover printed by A2 Reprographics
Ammex Park, Johnstown, Carmarthen.

Printed in Great Britain by **intype**
Woodman Works, Durnsford Road, Wimbledon SW19 8DR

FROM AN EDITOR'S DESK ....   Contents

Additional Contributors:

Iris Bryce has been a freelance writer for nearly forty years and is the author of the 'canal-boat' series *Canals Are My Home, Canals Are My Life, Canals Are My World* and *Canal Boat Cookery* . Her latest book *Remember Greenwich* was published in 1995.

Merric Davidson is a literary agent and organiser of the UK's largest prize for short stories, the Ian St James Awards. He also publishes *Acclaim* magazine featuring the short-listed entries.

Peter Finch, Manager of Oriel Bookshop in Cardiff, 'is arguably the most important small press poet-publisher-editor of the past twenty years' (*British Book News*) with several published collections of poems to his credit. He is also the author of *How To Publish Your Poetry* and *How To Publish Yourself* (Allison & Busby) and *The Poetry Business* (Seren).

Christine Hall is a widely published journalist and editor having worked for newspapers, trade and consumer magazines in the UK, Germany and China. Author of *How To Get A Job In Germany: How To Live & Work In China; How To Live & Work in Germany* and *How To Be A Freelance Journalist* (How To Books), she now runs Scriptease Editorial.

Lewis Hosegood is a creative writing tutor and author of *The Minotaur Garden* (Heinemann); *A Time Torn Man* (Heinemann); *The Birth Of Venus* (Hale); *Gabrielle & Other Stories* (Merlin Books); *No Worries & Other Stories* (Orlando) and *Portrait Of My Shadow* (Orlando).

Cass & Janie Jackson now operate the FLAIR Network for writers having had wide experience as editors and freelance writers in both national and specialist magazines. Cass has been widely published in children's literature and is the Director of Studies at the Academy of Children's Writers and the Guild of Romantic Writers. Janie has published three books for children, two romances and umpteen articles on a wide variety of subjects. She is also a senior tutor at the Academy of Children's Writers and Guild of Romance Writers.

Don Measham & Bob Windsor co-edit and publish *Staple Magazine,* one of the finest UK literary showcases for poets and fiction writers. Having been colleagues in the Matlock College English Department for many years, they have worked (unpaid) on the magazine, its competitions and small press publications since 1983.

Moe Sherrard-Smith is a tutor, manuscript assessor, literary agent and co-author (with Frederick E. Smith author of 38 novels, including the *633 Squadron* series) of *Write A Successful Novel*.

Nancy Smith is author of *Writing Your Life Story, The Fiction Writer's Handbook* (both by Piatkus) and *The Essential A-Z of Creative Writing*. As well as writing numerous story stories, articles and a novel (under a pen name) Nancy is a well-known and popular writing tutor and joint founder of the new Writer's Advice Centre's team.

Graham Stevenson is a prolific article/features writer and columnist; author of *How To Make Money Out of Writing* (Gower); *How To Win Consumer Competitions* (Kogan Page)and *The Dreamer's Guide to Winning the Big Competition Prizes* (Breese Books) in addition to having had over 200 articles and short stories published in over 40 magazines. His specialist subject is small business and he writes a regular column for *Yes,* the business magazine.

and from the Small Presses:
Elizabeth Baines & Ailsa Cox, joint editors of *Metropolitan* : **Andy Cox,** editor of *The Third Alternative* and *Zene* Magazine : **Derek Gregory,** Editor of the *Tees Valley WRITER*

Grateful acknowledgement must also go to Susan Alison, Victor Brown, Peggy Chapman-Andrews, Ann Cook, John Copley, Kate Dean, Barbara Horsfall, Abi Hughes-Edwards, Margaret Finch, Pamela Jorgensen, Leo Llewellyn, Trevor Lockwood, Lynne Patrick, Shirley Read, Gill Redman, Bernard Towler, Gal Travis, Lyn Westerman, Val Whitmarsh and Beryl Williams for their permission to quote from articles previously published in *Quartos Magazine*.

About the Author

From An Editor's Desk ... is an easy to follow, practical nuts-and-bolts guide to starting a creative writing career. Based on nearly ten year's experience as Editor of *Quartos Magazine*, Suzanne Ruthven draws on the advice of the many contributors, tutors and authors whose work has appeared in the publication.

Born in Northampton in 1952, Ruthven gained a broad experience in advertising & public relations, company administration and the conference industry before moving to Wales to concentrate on her own writing interests. She is a frequent contributor to a variety of UK publications and writes a regular column for two American magazines.

The first issue of *Quartos* appeared in 1987 and has since evolved into one of the most popular creative writing magazines in the UK with the emphasis very much on personal contact with the readership. Her first full-length, non-fiction book, *Malleus Satani - The Hammer of Satan*, an expose on modern witchcraft, was published in 1994 and her first novel *Whittlewood* is due for publication in spring 1996.

Chapter One   From an Editor's Desk ...

For anyone deciding to embark on a career in creative writing, the choice appears to fall between enrolling on an expensive correspondence course, or muddling along on your own. Writing as a potential vocation can be a costly and futile business if you're not warned of the pitfalls in advance.

It is also important for the beginner to realise that since becoming recognised as part of the vast money-earning leisure industry, creative writing is now providing a wide assortment of business opportunities for the entrepreneurial minded. As a result, all sorts of people are jumping on the literary bandwagon.

There are currently hundreds of how-to booklets, magazines, critique and assessment services, newsletters, writers' organisations and postal groups that have mushroomed in recent years, and many will disappear just as rapidly. All require subscriptions to survive ... but just how does the beginner ascertain which is going to provide practical nuts-and-bolts advice, and which serve to merely massage the combined egos of editor, author or tutor?

Everyone, we are now led to believe, can learn to write publishable/ saleable material - for a fee - and in recent years, it appears that anyone who has a published book or series of articles to their credit (or judged a literary competition), is eligible for weekend tutoring, workshops and courses.

Like most areas of craftsmanship, however, the master craftsman is not necessarily the best teacher, as one of our readers found to his cost: "I also discovered the fact that an author has written 50 books doesn't necessarily make him competent to talk about the subject," he wrote in a 'Letter to the Editor'.

Writing is a *craft* and as such, it must be honed and perfected much like the skill of marquetry or lace-making - it takes a great deal of time and study before a writer can expect to earn money from his/her work. Having won the school essay prize for a dissertation on the works of Balzac, or the breeding cycle of the damsel fly, does not mean you have the potential to become a future Booker nominee or an award winning journalist. Of course, the rudiments of grammar, spelling and syntax are necessary but the ability to transform basic English into highly commercial prose is a skill that must be learned.

That this simple philosophy is ignored by many aspiring writers is borne out by the vast numbers of unsolicited and unsuitable manuscripts that pass through the in-tray at *Quartos Magazine*. Multiply this by the total number of magazine and book publishers in the U.K alone and it produces a staggering amount of unsolicited material totally unsuitable for any of those individual publications or book lists. This vast sea of unwanted paper is sloshing around editorial offices throughout the country, just waiting for someone to return it to its anxious owner - who should never have sent it out in the first place!

Why does this happen?

Because the guilty parties will not accept that it is necessary for them to learn the craft before submitting work. All but a few refuse to acknowledge the fact that developing a successful writing career is 75% of knowing *beforehand* where to send it and only 25% writing. Lengthy letters and telephone conversations repeatedly betray the amateur's reluctance to become proficient in the most important discipline of creative writing - *market research*. Most have been mistakenly led to believe that publication is there for the asking and that they have nothing further to learn.

What's in the Quartos postbag?

The weekly intake of unsolicited poetry collections can range from one poem to whole anthologies from unknown writers, with covering letters requesting criticism and advice on where to submit them next. Unless there is a rare collection of really exciting poetry, most will be returned with a rejection letter and a set of guidelines, providing a stamped addressed envelope has been enclosed for the purpose.

Unsolicited fiction fares little better - but the bundles are invariably larger. "I enclose my story for publication in your magazine," is not going to invoke any constructive comments from any editor or publisher's reader. They haven't asked for it; don't want to read it and don't have the time for pleasantries ... so unless an adequately stamped addressed envelope has been enclosed for its return, it's doubtful whether the author is ever going to see the manuscript again.

Bald letters asking: "Do you give advice on novels, please? Please send details?" Details of what? Advice on suitable reading matter for mature adults? What's going to win the next Whitbread Prize?

"I would be obliged if you would comment on my story and suggest any alterations," is the most frequent request for free advice and can accompany anything from a 1000 word story to a full length novel. Would you take your car into the garage to be repaired and not expect to pay for the mechanic's time?

"Can you tell me where to send the enclosed short stories as I need the money?" Curl fingers and resist the urge to be facetious.

In addition, editors, like librarians, have to cope with an assortment of 'strangenesses' enclosed in the envelope along with the manuscripts. One short story turned up saturated in grease, as if the writer had kept half a pound of bacon wrapped in it for a week. Needless to say it was returned unread, with a brief but polite note to the effect that it was unacceptable in that state.

The folded sheets of paper contain all sorts of surprises for the unwary - teeth from a comb, knots of human hair, nail pairings and even a tuft of pubic hair! Manuscripts arrive, in the form of a carbon copy that suggests they came into existence around the time of the second Punic Wars and are completely illegible ... smeared runic messages on yellowing paper. It is inexcusable to send an Editor a two page A4 letter which continues around all eight margins and hope for a sensible reply!

Finding Your Way Around:

Editing *Quartos* since 1987 has provided the opportunity to study on a weekly, closely monitored scale (i.e. a low circulation, privately owned publication), what must be magnified a hundred-fold on a daily basis in the offices of the publishing giants. We have also built up a productive information exchange with our regular contributors, most of whom are published authors in their own right - alongside their tutorial duties with local Further Education programmes, correspondence schools or regional workshops. Finally, having an Editor with independent writing interests, the magazine can benefit from valuable insights into writing for publication from differing standpoints.

Subscribers are asked to indicate which areas of writing interest them most, providing us with a constantly updated picture of current trends. Since the readership is large enough to give a valid census reading, our latest figures show that the greatest national interest (over 50%) lies in fiction - where there are the fewest market opportunities for the freelancer.

Results of the Quartos Creative Writing Census 1995:

Short Stories - irrespective of genre:	34.5%
Novels:	18.0%
Technical and general interest articles:	24.0%
Poetry:	17.25%
Writing for TV/Radio/Stage:	4.0%
A general interest in Children's/Teenage fiction:	1.75%
Specific interest in biography:	0.5%

Another significant point is that the majority of freelance writers have more than one interest. The would-be novelist fills in the remaining hours with poetry; the features writer dabbles in television drama on the side; the short story writer also turns his/her hand to articles or local history. Children's writing and biography usually provide writers with a secondary string to their bow. Very few writers concentrate on one particular area, thereby increasing their chances of acceptance and publication in one field or another.

The majority of submissions accepted for publication in *Quartos* come from regular readers, consisting mainly of non-fiction i.e writing-related articles. Often material diversifies into humour and our popular *Vellum* page enables writers to wax lyrical about a favourite author. The regular fiction pages feature the winning entries from previous readers' short story competitions. Rejection of material is *usually* on the grounds that a similar piece has already been accepted and is being held on file, or a repeat of what's been featured before. This abnormally high acceptance rate is due to our readers getting to know the likes and foibles of their Editor - in other words, they know their market-place.

An Editor's personal writing interests can also provide another insight into publishing but just because you're editing a popular writers' magazine doesn't mean that your highly prized fictional offering will be guaranteed acceptance elsewhere. Unless you're in the Archer, Burchill, Cooper bracket, rejections are still a regular occurrence. Which just goes to prove that no matter how well you know the publishing industry, you can still expect to have your work rejected if it's not in tune with current editorial/publisher's policy.

Being asked to judge other organisations' writing competitions gives a fair indication of the standard of work that an extremely wide cross-section of writers (some with many year's experience) consider 'polished' enough to enter for competition. A good half of the manuscripts received by competition organisers should never have left the writer's desk, and, if a judge has rashly agreed to read the entire entry there's an awful lot of hair tearing to be done before the finalists are selected. One judge recently received a

11

bundle of over 4000 poems from which to make a final selection of five prize winners!

Accepting invitations to take part in writers' workshops also provides illuminating experience for the regular tutor, especially if students have been given the opportunity to submit examples of their work beforehand for assessment. Often the same faces, year after year, eagerly devouring the information but still no nearer publication.

One gets the feeling that by attending regular workshops, many can justify their claim to be a writer, even if their only publishing success to date is the parish magazine. Other students can be openly hostile, because you're not telling them what they want to hear. On the plus side, tutors have the opportunity to meet some very talented new-comers, and can derive a great deal of satisfaction from seeing these names begin to appear quite regularly in the small press magazines as experience and confidence are gained.

An Editor's in-tray becomes the focal point for all sorts of contacts from other editors, writers, Regional Arts Boards, societies and organisations. This is where we pick up grapevine gossip (much of which we can't use); warning against the editors who don't pay up, agents who lose manuscripts, publishers who don't answer letters and magazines that go bust, having pocketed the subscription money. New magazines and organisations blossom, dozens of writers wither under the strain and *still* the voracious creative writing industry rolls on.

As with any other profession, however, there are long established organisations for writers, and once the beginner has found his/her feet, it can be advantageous to join one or two to keep a finger on the pulse of your particular writing interest. Some associate fees are as low as £10 per year - although these increase once you've become a published author. *Quartos* is a member of the following and draws on the information passed around in the various newsletters to keep its readership abreast of current publishing news:

The Society of Authors : The Gothic Society :
The Welsh Academy : The Author-Publisher Network

12

The two main writers' handbooks (*The Writer's Handbook* and *The Writers' & Artists' Yearbook*) list the majority of well-known professional associations and societies covering most aspects of writing activities, plus a good selection of literary societies. If you are interested in a particular organisation (i.e. The Comedy Writers' Association, New Playwrights' Trust, the Romantic Novelists' Association, Society of Women Writers & Journalists, Women Writers' Network, etc.) don't be put off by the fact that you're a beginner. The membership secretary will be only too pleased to inform you of the nomination requirements and many societies do offer associate membership for unpublished writers.

So what is a successful writer?

Personally speaking, I would say that anyone who makes a living, or earns a *reasonable second income* through writing is successful. Readers frequently ask why there are no 'proper writers', i.e. famous names, amongst the *Quartos* contributors - 'names' demand high fees and we can't afford them.

The majority of writers featured in the magazine *are* successful - the names might not be recognisable, but between them they have quite an impressive range of titles to their credit from publishing houses like Piatkus, Allison & Busby, Hale, Gower, Seren, Heinemann, etc; not to mention those who produce technical/ educational books through less well known publishers.

Literary agent, Moe Sherrard-Smith picked up on this point immediately. "I smiled about *Quartos* contributors not being 'proper writers' - I'm often denigrated in the same way. Yet we who tutor, write a diversity of books and associated material (in my case the writing textbook; a *Guide to the Yorkshire Air Museum*; in the past, three poetry volumes; and thousands of newspaper and magazine articles from my days as a magazine and newspaper editor; and invariably turn out around 40,000 finished words per week) are not seen to be as established, since the zenith of achievement seems to be a novel on the bookshelves."

Since most of the contributors featured in *From An Editor's Desk* are writing tutors as well as authors, several were asked what they had found were the most common misconceptions held by those new to the writing game ...

Lewis Hosegood:

"I would say that it's a lazy, or at least timid, attitude towards the essential nature of revision. So often, having (admittedly) slaved over a lengthy piece, they are reluctant to cut, re-write, re-arrange or just start all over again. Some even take the rather arrogant view that first thoughts are best, and 'what I have written I have written', or 'I wouldn't want to alter a single word of my masterpiece'. Of these two reactions one can sympathise with the first more than the second. Revision is a chore, but nowadays if we are lucky enough to have a word processor, much of the old sweat-and-tears can be eliminated. There's less excuse for pig-headed arrogance."

Janie Jackson:

"In our experience, most beginners have a strong resistance to any form of revision. They feel that once they have written their story, article or book, the words are set in concrete and cannot be changed. Faced with the information that Ernest Hemingway once re-wrote a first chapter 39 times, most new writers turn a whiter shade of pale and retreat. Another equally common misconception is that there is no need to study the markets. Indeed, a lot of new writers have never even heard of market research. They work on the assumption that "if a story is good enough to be published, it will be accepted", blithely ignoring the fact that, for example, a fishing magazine is unlikely to be interested in romantic fiction."

Cass Jackson:

"Most new writers get a nasty shock when they discover that writing is HARD WORK and that, as with all other crafts, they need to serve an apprenticeship. Their reaction is either to quit or to keep on writing in the same old way, regardless of the advice and then complain that 'publishers are not fair, they don't give new writers a chance'.

14

Having said that, I would also add that almost anyone who can write a good letter is capable of producing one article or story and getting it published. This is probably because their enthusiasm for that first idea/topic brings their writing to vivid life. It is only after they collect a few rejections that they begin to realise that there is more to writing than simply stringing words together."

Moe Sherrard-Smith:

"The most common misconception beginners have of creative writing is that anyone who can scribble a letter to Auntie Mary can create short stories and novels which publishers will not only pay vast sums of money for, but which they will also fight over. It's true that the greater majority of tyro novelists and students all feel that a book simply happens because they have an idea. As a result of this, so many of them fail as they lack any clear concept of the structure of a plot and how the creation of character works. A misconception that arises, I feel, from that old truism 'easy reading has meant hard writing'."

Lewis Hosegood:

"How many beginners are capable of penning a saleable manuscript without some inside knowledge of the marketplace? I would answer practically none. Frequently I ask my students, 'Who are you writing for?' Very often it's for themselves. Well, that's all right if they're prepared to stop there. If they want to see it in print, however, they must definitely study the markets. If it's intended as a magazine piece, it is imperative they read the magazine first - from cover to cover, including the advertisements, and preferably over several issues."

Nancy Smith:

"Beginners often find it hard to accept that writing is, in fact, a craft and, as such, there are 'rules' which need to be learned. Studying the market is a fundamental principle for success. Writing articles, short stories or even novels with no idea of the market aimed for, is almost guaranteed to bring rejection. Every editor says the same thing: the most common fault, resulting in manuscripts being turned down, is that the writer has clearly not studied the market to assess fundamentals such as length, style and content."

Lewis Hosegood:

"My advice to the raw beginner? Try to write something every day, even if it's only a few thoughts or a diary entry. Don't worry about writer's block - we all suffer from it. Just get on with something else. The point is, the more you write the better you will get. At anything."

Nancy Smith:

"The best advice for a raw beginner is to keep in mind the adage WRITE ABOUT WHAT YOU KNOW. Draw on your own experience and 'milk' it for all it's worth. Concentrate on writing articles rather than short stories at the start, as these can be easier to sell. Build up self-confidence in your writing ability in this way, before attempting the more demanding fiction. But, above all, be prepared to learn your craft, persevere and never give up."

Moe Sherrard-Smith:

"I would urge beginners to spend a great deal of time considering the theme and plot of the novel before rushing to the typewriter or WP. It's a rare author who can work without a full synopsis which has addressed the outline of the story and ensured that the author has the confidence to embark on a long and lonely slog to the final page. Too many beginners start with a rush of hot blood over a single idea, believing it will be sufficient basis for a complete book and the characters will then take over and write the story, only to have the novel fizzle out after a few chapters, lacking drive, ideas or steam.

As an agent and a publisher's reader, I see far too many of the latter kind of script. These waste everyone's time and exhaust patience. Sadly, their speedy rejection also leads to a great deal of disappointment for the author. A dressmaker wouldn't send out a dress randomly cut from different patterns and with bits tacked together, or sleeves set in the waist: Some novel scripts are constructed a bit like that!"

So Where Do I Begin?

Firstly, NOT by enrolling on an expensive postal writing course or spending a fortune on 'how-to' books. During the initial stages of a writing career it is doubtful whether any beginner will know for certain which direction his/her writing will take, so wait until you have a more sharply defined concept before shelling out any cash. You may have an idea of what you *want* to write but until you have explored all the different avenues your writing *can take*, it would be unwise to hold firmly to the belief that there is a budding novelist, short story writer or investigative journalist is the making.

By investing in a couple of regular creative writing magazines, the beginner will have the opportunity to see which one offers them the widest scope for novices. Not only should they include informative articles on all aspects of creative writing, it is a good idea to look for the magazines offering in-house competitions, a diversity of useful material and value for money. No doubt you will prefer the format of one and the content of another, so choose whichever offers the *right sort of information for you*, i.e. easy to follow instructions or opportunities. Most of the magazines include pieces on all aspects of fiction and non-fiction writing, as well as poetry and script-writing. Some contain more market information than others; some offer more in-depth competition news; while others lean more towards celebrity-written know-how.

What they all *should* do, is to start the beginner thinking about intended market outlets. Most run regular competitions for their readers to encourage them to try out their writing skills under the auspices of that particular editor (who may occasionally offer constructive criticism of individual submissions). The current edition of *The Writer's Handbook* and *The Writers' & Artists' Yearbook* gives up-to-date information on these monthly/bi-monthly publications. Most UK writing magazines are only available on

17

subscription so, before deciding on which one to buy, send for a sample issue of each to study, at your leisure.

The Writer's Bookshelf:

The second most important expenditure is the purchase of the essential writer's reference books which should always be kept within easy reach of your desk or work-station. (Forget how-to books for the moment - these will be covered in the next chapter). Go for *The Writer's Handbook* and/or *The Writers' & Artists' Year Book* which give details of editorial, agency and publisher's requirements, plus a wealth of valuable advice by seasoned writers. Before making your decision pop along to the Public Library's Reference Section or local bookshop and examine them for yourself. If you can afford it, buy both.

Next, the best dictionary you can afford; pocket ones are fine but a writer often needs more information than these can provide. My own favourite is a 1899 etymological dictionary which has seen better days, but rarely fails to come up with the required spelling. A copy of *Roget's Thesaurus* should never be far away from any writer's hand, since it can always be relied upon to produce that alternative word or expression. Your encyclopedia does not need to be an expensive edition of *Britannica* - the old children's set in the attic will do, and can provide thousands of ideas, cross references, less common snippets of information or historical anecdote to liven up your articles and stories; bear in mind that quite a few subjects have an independent encyclopedia to cover it.

A writer can never possess too many reference books - these make ideal presents from friends and family - collect as many different books of quotations as you have room for, since they are extremely useful in sparking off ideas for a title or subject. *The Book of Similes* can be equally as informative - as can *The Penguin Dictionary of Historical Slang* and *Brewer's Dictionary of Phrase and Fable*. If you have a penchant for foreign words and phrases, then *A Concise Dictionary of Foreign Expressions* can give added flavour (and **exact** meanings) - or *Nil Desperandum* for Latin tags and phrases. Books giving the origins of both surnames and first names are valuable additions to your collection; another indispensable publication (now sadly out of print but usually traceable through a reliable book-search) is *An Encyclopedia of World History*.

Of course you could manage without vast numbers of reference books, particularly if you live near a good Public Library, but it is convenient to have as many as possible handy for the moment you need them. There is nothing more annoying than having to wait until your next visit to the library if an essential piece of information is eluding your memory. If you live in a rural area where the library van only visits once a week, or you have to rely on a small sub-library, it could be a months before you can get your hands on a particularly relevant volume.

As an alternative, cultivate a relationship with your local second-hand book dealer; the sort of chap who operates from a market stall is best for obtaining out -of-date reference works which still have a lot of mileage left for the writer. Make a point of regular visits to the stall and keep an eye open for old editions of *Pears Cyclopedia*. (I keep one for every decade so when I needed to know the population of Peru in the 1950s, the information was readily to hand.) Similarly, out-of-print editions of *Debrett, Who's Who, Who Was Who*, etc. are useful, and your dealer will keep them for you if you are a regular customer, since this type of book is normally trashed and never put on the stalls.

Natural history books of all kinds are invaluable, especially those which give details of localised/seasonal flora and fauna. All of the above can provide endless material for articles, features and fictional backgrounds once you get started.

There may come a time when you need to acquire more specialist material than can be provided by your local library, or perhaps the books you require are now out of print. Pick up a copy of *Book & Magazine Collector* from the local newsagent and go through the 'for sale' listings, place an advertisement yourself, or contact one of the numerous national book-searches with details of your requirements. However, do make **sure** the one you choose clearly states that there is no search fee - or you could land up with a heavy bill and no book!

Last but not least, invest in a LARGE desk diary - one that gives a week at a glance and has plenty of pages for notes. Use this to keep track of all your submissions, rejections, acceptances, competition closing dates, reminders, and ideas for articles and stories. Although *Quartos* is fully documented on computer, I still use the desk diary system as an instantly accessible and transportable record of all my writing and personal activities. Some of the larger business diaries also carry a section for accounts, which should be perfectly adequate for your initial income/expenditure details.

The Information Highway:

Information is the key-word to success for all writers. The beginner would be well advised to work initially within the guidelines given by most writing courses: Write about what you know. Using and building on personal experience as a background for both fiction and non-fiction lends depth to the work and reflects the writer's confidence in his/her subject. This inside knowledge enables you to add new dimensions to description, or to include a snippet of fresh detail which gives added zest to the manuscript.

Once you've gained more experience and confidence, the secret is to turn the advice of 'writing from experience' on its head. In *Interviewing for Journalists*, author Joan Clayton states: "... a journalist doesn't need to know anything about anything; s/he merely needs to know WHERE TO FIND OUT. Being an investigator is a paramount journalistic skill." This advice applies to ALL writers, so develop the habit of acquiring information as a second nature; start by investing in *Research for Writers* by Ann Hoffmann, which lists nearly every reference source you're likely to need.

Many people are intimidated by the Reference Section of their local Public Library, but this shouldn't be the case. If unfamiliar with your surroundings, ask the librarian for the books in question and s/he will locate them for you, as titles in the Reference Section are not available for loan; there may be another copy in the main lending library, so ask the librarian to check. If you're not a regular visitor to the Reference Library, try this simple exercise: Ask for copies of *The Writer's Handbook, The Writers' & Artists' Yearbook* and *Willing's Press Guide*. Half an hour spent examining these three titles will convince any beginner about the amount of potential market outlets for well-written material.

Getting Technical:

The majority of writing books cast the question of purchasing a word processor/personal computer in a minor role, but speaking from an editorial point of view, I find that over 80% of the manuscripts submitted for consideration are now produced on a WP/PC, even those from beginners. At the start of their career, few writers appreciate just how many times it will be necessary to re-type a manuscript before it is ready for submission, and a WP/PC can save a considerable amount of time and frustration.

Most of us begin writing on an old and trusted typewriter, but if you are thinking of investing in a new machine, perhaps you should spare a moment to consider the long-term advantages of a WP/PC. Of course, if you don't intend to indulge your new hobby any further than the occasional competition entry or short story, then a typewriter will be adequate. On the other hand, if your intentions are more ambitious, then a WP/PC is certainly a better investment than an electric typewriter.

A WP/PC dispenses with a lot of time consuming work, especially when it comes to editing a full-length manuscript. Instead of hand-written alterations - or "It will have to go out as it is!" - two minutes will remove or alter the offending word, paragraph or sentence, and a far neater job arrives on the editor's desk. This does not mean, however, that a poorly written WP/PC submission is looked upon any more favourably than one turned out on an old manual typewriter, even though presentation is an important aspect of the writer's work.

In the early days *Quartos* was produced on a bottom of the range Amstrad; in addition to this, the PC coped extremely well with a full sized novel, two house journals, numerous short stories and articles. Everything was available at the push of a button, with the added bonus of not having the chore of re-typing whenever you wished to alter a manuscript for re-submission. It also meant there were no carbon copies lying around waiting to be filed, not to mention personal correspondence, addresses and mailing lists.

Apart from having to part with the cash, there is only one fly in the literary ointment when it comes down to acquiring a WP/PC - it is still almost impossible to decipher the instruction manuals, especially if you are computer illiterate. This obstacle can be overcome by two different approaches. The first (and easiest) is to purchase the equipment and software from an appointed computer dealer. Having explained what *you* require of the WP/PC and its software, the entire package can be purchased with the programme installed and ready for operation. Some dealers will even give a couple of hour's tuition and remain 'on call' if you feel the need to indulge in a bit of hysteria because some strange message keeps appearing on the screen to tell you that you're doing something wrong, but not why or how to correct it.

You pay a little more buying from a dealer than for the alternative choice, which is to buy from a high street shop or 'Cash & Carry' at a lower price and use the WP/PC telephone help-lines. The disadvantage with the latter, is that it is probably a long distance call during peak-period and the telephone bill can mount up very quickly if your problem isn't easily resolved. Added to this, you will not be communicating in the same language because 'computer-speak' is almost unintelligible to the uninitiated. You could land up by putting the difference in price in the pocket of British Telecom. So, unless you have a good friend who's a computer buff, my recommendation is the local dealer; pay the extra for the privilege of driving him round the bend and if he doesn't provide this service - buy from someone who does ...

... So now you've got the thing home and probably suffering from buyer's remorse but if your intention is to become a serious and dedicated writer with lots of irons in the editorial fire, consider that it is now possible to have everything you're working on, available at the touch of a finger - even if it's only the title and a few lines of rough notes. You have the idea - type it in and save it. It doesn't matter that it might be necessary to change the whole thing around at a later stage. When revamping an article originally intended for one publication, 10-15 minutes can alter the angle of the whole subject and slant the piece from a completely different viewpoint. Would you go to so much trouble if you had to completely re-type it?

If your long-term plan is to produce a novel, non-fiction, biography or any full-length work, then a WP/PC is a must. So many writers have slaved away at a typewriter, wasting reams of paper, typing the first thing that came into their heads, only to find at the end, the work had more holes than Emmenthal cheese; the work was not long enough (or too long) for a standard publisher's format; or the bubbles had gone out of the brilliant and witty dialogue. So they RETYPE. The story begins to develop the semblance of a decent plot, but after re-reading it, the author discovers that a fairly powerful character who stormed into Chapter 6 has disappeared without trace by Chapter 14. Added to this, he also discovers that he has unwittingly changed the spelling of the hero's name half way through ... RETYPE.

The author re-reads and is relatively happy but by this time he has developed word blindness - and anyway, it has to be RETYPED with double-spacing, correct margins, etc. For a first work, he might have saved a lot of time and heartache in having the first few chapters assessed by a professional. But ... back comes the manuscript with pages of instructions for improvement. Another RETYPE.

The instructions completed, the manuscript is sent off to an agent or publisher who writes back to say: 'yes ... but ... or maybe', and again the novel is RETYPED (unless the writer has decided to commission a service agency). After six months the manuscript has been returned with a letter saying 'Sorry' and looks as though someone's dog has been at it. It can't be sent off to another publisher in that condition, so ... yes, you've guessed it. Even the most dedicated beginner would be put off by the though of having to type a full length novel SEVEN times!

Another advantage of using a WP/PC is that the writer only needs type the main body of the text once. True, it will be subjected to numerous alterations, additions and deletions but it will not be necessary to retype every single page over and over again. You can turn from chapter to chapter and see immediately how the alterations affect the overall plot.

If planning a non-fiction work, then the advantages are even greater - since the writer can type in all the basic research material in note form, typing up the chapters as the research is completed. If having got to the end, only to discover a new and exciting source that must be included, it can be simply done without a complete re-type. When you stop to consider how many times any piece of writing needs re-working (even an article or short story) before it is fit for an editor/publisher's eye, the advantages come out way in favour of a WP/PC.

It is, however, important to understand the implications behind modern technology before making a purchase. Most reputable dealers will have a selection of programmes already installed on their demonstration machines, so ask to see them in operation. What you are looking for is a software package that is easy to use; will provide you with standard A4 single and double-spaced copy, as well as the facility to produce text on disk in ASCII or TEXT format (internationally recognised systems which can be read by almost every publisher's computer anywhere in the world), should a publisher/editor request it.

The package should also provide a reasonable spell-check and, more importantly, an easily accessible word count facility. Don't be fooled by packages that offer a vast dictionary and thesaurus - having had a thesaurus installed, it's never been on the screen, because I continue to use *Roget's* version in book form for convenience. Also, many of the software packages don't always recognise prefixes and suffixes which a good etymological dictionary provides. Beware of American spellings, too.

In *The Electronic Author* (a Society of Author's publication) one of the member's letters also warns against assuming that the larger the built-in dictionary for spell-checking, the better the package.

"The reality is that a 10,000-word dictionary will alert you to more slips than will a 100,000-word dictionary. To illustrate this, imagine that you intend to type 'western' and by mistake typed 'wester'. The smaller dictionary would be likely to query it, whereas the bumper version would let it pass."

Grapevine gossip indicates that before too long, manuscripts will only be considered by publishers and features editors if submissions are available on computer disk. To support this claim, I've already had the experience of both American and UK publishers asking for a full length manuscripts to be submitted - but only if the hard copy (i.e. the printed paper version) was accompanied by the complete work on disk in compatible format! I also have a non-fiction book that is currently being prepared for 'electronic publishing' which means that the text is available anywhere in the world through computer access. Like all aspects of business, the publishing world will be keeping abreast of new technology. Whether we like it or not, the computer is here to stay.

One last word of warning - if tempted to invest in a new electronic typewriter, word processor or personal computer system, **don't** part with your old machine until you've mastered the intricacies of the new one. One of our readers spent so much time poring over the manual instead of getting on with her novel, that it almost destroyed the creative urge completely.

Recommended Reading:

A general purpose how-to book that can be extremely useful at this stage is Chriss McCallum's *How To ... Write For Publication* (How-To Books) which contains a lot of practical advice on getting started, preparing and submitting your work, writing for competitions, magazines and newspapers. She also examines self-financed publishing, general non-fiction and fiction writing. With plenty of additional information on specialist markets, there are also details of the various services, associations and societies open to unpublished writers. ISBN 1-85703-041-9

Chapter Two   Schools of Thought

Having familiarised yourself with a basic introduction to the complex world of creative writing through the services of a writers' magazine, it may now be worth considering joining a group or organisation which will offer some form of help in ironing out some of the initial problems of getting into print.

Perhaps you just need someone to provide some outside stimulus or friendly criticism. You may have already changed direction from your original concept of story-teller or journalist. Or there may be the need for some constructive tuition. Whatever your goal, this is not the time to pay out considerable sums of money for tuition.

Before doing anything else, contact the Literature Officer of your **Regional Arts Board**. Most of the RABs organise activities for local writers by way of festivals, workshops and discussion groups run by established writers and poets from within the region - all at very little cost to the writer. The Regional Arts Boards encourage new writers so why not consider supporting them, since it could be to your advantage to receive advance notice of any literary events in the area.

Most RABs can also provide a list of regionally based writers' circles, while several produce regular newsletters of local literary interest, in addition to writers' information packs. If you are unsure which RAB covers your area, send a s.a.e. to The Literature Department of **The Arts Council of Great Britain,** 14 Great Peter Street, London SW1P 3NQ; **The Scottish Arts Council,** 12 Manor

Place, Edinburgh EH3 7DD or **The Welsh Arts Council**, Museum Place, Cardiff CF1 3NX and request further information. Alternatively contact your local Literature Officer at the Regional Arts Board direct, enclosing a stamped addressed envelope for a prompt reply and request that your name be placed on their mailing list.

Cleveland Arts
7-9 Eastbourne Road, Linthorpe, Middlesbrough,
Cleveland TS5 6QS

Eastern Arts Board
Cherry Hinton Hall, Cherry Hinton Road, Cambridge CB1 4DW

East Midlands Arts
Mountfields House, Loughborough, Leicestershire LE11 3HU

London Arts
Elme House, 133 Long Acre, Covent Garden, London WC2E 3HU

Northern Arts
9-10 Osbourne Terrace, Jesmond, Newcastle Upon Tyne NE2 1NZ

North West Arts
12 Harter Street, Manchester M1 6HY

Southern Arts
13 St. Clements Street, Winchester SO23 9DQ

South East Arts
10 Mount Ephraim, Tunbridge Wells, Kent TN4 8AS

South West Arts
Bradninch Place, Gandy Street, Exeter EX4 3LS

West Midlands Arts
82 Granville Street, Birmingham N1 2LH

Yorkshire & Humberside Arts
21 Bond Street, Dewsbury, West Yorkshire WF13 1AX

North Wales Arts
10 Wellfield House, Bangor, Gwynedd LL57 1ER

South East Wales Arts
Victoria Street, Cwmbran, Gwent NP44 3YT

West Wales Arts
3 Red Street, Carmarthen, Dyfed SA31 1QL

If contacting **The Arts Council of Northern Ireland** (185 Stanmills Road, Belfast BT9 5DU) you can use British stamps for a reply but when writing to **The Arts Council of Ireland** (70 Merrion Square, Dublin 2) you will need to enclose International Reply Coupons (IRCs) which are obtainable from main Post Offices.

Correspondence Tuition:

The first contact many would-be writers have with the creative writing world is via the advertisements for correspondence courses which regularly appear in the national press. During the years of editing *Quartos*, we have received numerous letters questioning the effectiveness of correspondence courses and although the debate goes on, the following observations appear to be valid. Correspondence courses can be:

(a) a sorry disappointment;
(b) a worthwhile investment;
or
(c) a downright waste of money.

On the first count, having paid the fees, the new writer ploughs through a series of poorly photocopied exercises which are corrected by a tutor who appears to offer neither constructive advice nor criticism, and who inspires little or no confidence with his: "No luck with that one? Well, let's get on to something else," attitude.

At the end of the course the writer has sold nothing to cover his/ her expenditure, nor gained any worthwhile instruction.

With (b) it can considered an investment if the student knuckles down to the work set out in well written exercises *and* establishes a rapport with the tutor. The more expensive courses usually guarantee that students will earn what they've spent in fees before the end of the course; if they haven't, they will refund the fee in full. Needless to say, you must complete the course before presenting yourself as a failure.

Of course (c) will be a waste of money because the writer never gets around to finishing the course. In fact, it is quite common for a beginner to enrol on a course and having paid the fee, shove the initial exercise in a drawer with the thought: "I'll keep that for the winter months," or "I'll wait till the kids start school," which is as far as they get. By the time Lesson One surfaces again, the budding writer has either lost interest completely, or has had some measure of success and doesn't want to go back to basics. It has also been suggested on many occasions, that many writing schools make their profits out of the drop-outs!

Janie Jackson has been a correspondence school tutor with The Academy of Children's Writers and The Guild of Romantic Writers for many years and was able to offer the following comments from the other side of the marker pen:

Janie Jackson:

"Have you ever considered taking a correspondence course?" Very few writers can honestly answer 'no' to that question, and there's a lot to be said in favour of getting some expert tuition in your chosen craft. Certainly the advertisements are tempting. It's also true that though the fees may be in the region of £200, you could recoup the money by selling three or four articles or short stories. But can you be sure that you will get a stream of acceptances as a result of taking the course?

Much depends on your tutor, of course, and it's important that you should be realistic about what you can expect from him. For a start, it is unlikely that he will be a famous author. Let's face it - a tutor works for a correspondence school because he needs to supplement his income. Best selling writers don't have this need. When you receive your tutor's c.v. you may be disappointed to find that he has worked mainly for small publications. Don't allow this to deter you. What matters to you is his *teaching* ability, his *enthusiasm* for the task and his *patience* with students.

Make no mistake - a tutor needs patience. You'd be surprised how many students assume that in enrolling for a correspondence course they have hired a full-time critic for all submitted work. Do you realise that your tutor is paid per assignment? Don't expect him to comment on extra-curricular work *unless* he has previously agreed to do so. On more than one occasion a student has been hurt and offended when I've returned unread the 10,000 word manuscript he has asked me to 'glance' at.

Nevertheless, I'm always upset if I lose a student's confidence and trust, because the tutor/student relationship is so important. If you find that you're not on the same wavelength as your tutor, do ask to be transferred to somebody else. Don't be in too much of a hurry, however. It takes time for a student and tutor to settle down together. Some students regard compliments with deep suspicion and demand 'strong constructive criticism'; others wilt at the merest breath of adverse comment and beg for 'more encouragement'. The tutor has to steer a middle course between these two extremes. If he doesn't get it absolutely right with your first assignment, don't rush to demand a replacement.

Tutors love enthusiastic students, of course. But don't be so keen that you send him Exercise Two a couple of days after you've dispatched Exercise One. It makes sense to wait for the return of the first typescript before submitting the next. That way you benefit from the tutor's guidance.

DO stick to the designated assignments, too. A good correspondence course is carefully structured to gradually stretch the student's abilities. If you ignore the set exercises, submitting what you feel like writing, you won't get the full benefit from the course. Your tutor will probably get impatient too, if you try to buck the system. Look at it this way: If you enrolled for a dressmaking course, you wouldn't expect to make an elaborate evening gown before you'd learned to tack the seams together. Why then expect to write a blockbuster novel before you've learned to construct a sentence correctly?

All this may sound as if the tutor can do no wrong. That's not so. There are poor tutors - there are even bad ones. But we're all human - and we appreciate courtesy and co-operation. Above all, we want to help you get the best possible value from the course for which you have enrolled."

Another of our correspondence school tutors, Val Whitmarsh, suggested that students who complain are possibly those who are disappointed that creative writing isn't as easy as they thought it would be. "Or perhaps they have simply bought the wrong course. For quite a number, a less demanding, less isolated evening class would be better - and cheaper!"

Moe Sherrard-Smith:

"No workshop or course, even one-to-one tuition via correspondence, or face-to-face, can teach you to write fiction if you lack inherent creativity. In the early days of writing, specifically so with novels, it is in the mechanical structure of the scaffolding - the plot - that writers need encouragement and objective advice. All forms of tuition can demonstrate techniques, point out weaknesses in plotting and characterisation. "

On the other side of the coin, however, there are the writing school horror stories similar to the one related by one of our readers who, whilst not having any complaint against her tutor, was less than happy with the outcome. The wording of the advertisement gave the impression that the student would not only be helped to place their work during the course, but assured a refund in the unlikely event that they had not recouped their course fees by the end of their studies. Having sold nothing on completing the course (despite a helpful and encouraging tutor), Pamela Jorgenson requested the refund of her fees.

"As I had written my original application while temporarily in Copenhagen, and my married name is 'foreign', I had been put on a simple course for foreign students, which was exempt from the money-back clause. I pointed out that this was an administrative mistake, since my original c.v showed me to be British and that I had no means of knowing that I'd been put in the wrong class. They still refused a refund, but offered me the proper, longer course (with the same tutor) at no extra cost."

Our would-be writer battled on for another two years, managing to sell a couple of articles, for very small fees, but had all her stories rejected, despite her tutor being unable to fault them. Whilst she hadn't recouped the original fees, she felt it was too much trouble to complain again. "The tutors are probably right when they say they have a lot to put up with from some of their students," she concluded, "though I have the feeling that *that* kind seldom last the whole course. But those students who are looking for advice on how to sell their work are in for a big disappointment. You're on your own out there!"

If you feel that you have the mental discipline right from the start to treat the course as a serious enterprise, find out from other writers which one they would recommend and, if given the opportunity, ask to have a look at the working papers before sending off any money. Don't just enrol on a correspondence course because you've seen an advertisement in a national magazine or newspaper - ask around first.

Having decided to go ahead, make sure that a few hours can be set aside each week to study and complete the exercises. Should the tutor make recommendation for alterations to your manuscript, act on it - don't push it to one side. Think very carefully whether you need to enrol on a full course which can cost anything up to £200+. If you are only interested in article and feature writing or short stories, then you possibly don't need the full course covering poetry, children's stories and the novel. Don't be afraid to ask if they run mini-courses; and don't be embarrassed to request details of any tutor's credentials.

One correspondence course that is rapidly making a name for itself is **REAL WRITERS** where the tutors are all working writers who each deal with just a handful of clients. This, founder Lynne Patrick informed *Quartos*, forms positive, productive and above all, individual relationships. The course operates on a pay-as-you-go system, so the clients get exactly what they pay for.

"There's no question of 'not finishing the course' because each consists of as many, or as few assignments as the client wants - from a single appraisal to ongoing support over several years."

The monthly deadline and word budget set for each assignment are REAL WRITERS' way of encouraging self-discipline. The tutors are all published, working writers and between them cover the wide spectrum of short and full length fiction, drama for stage, radio and television, fantasy, poetry and writing for children. In the first two years of operation their students have achieved high placings in several national competitions, ongoing publication in women's magazines for four different writers, a 100% acceptance rate for the four pieces submitted to various markets (including the BBC, a notoriously hard nut to crack) for another client; while several others have received considerable encouragement from editors and publishers.

"Not bad, considering most clients come to us with a nil success rate, and that we have a maximum of 35 people on our books at one time ... once they leave us they feel able to fend for themselves," Lynne Patrick concluded.

Discipline:

If *Information* is the first key-word for a writer, then the second must surely be *Discipline*. In this instance we are talking about the development of self-discipline; for if a writer is unable to control his or her own writing timetable, insurmountable difficulties can be experienced later on when it comes to working within deadlines and contracts imposed by others. This is one of the reasons why I personally maintain that joining a correspondence school immediately on thinking: "Ah, I think I'll take up creative writing," is not a good idea. To obtain the best results from a writing course (as with any other form of educational enterprise), it requires regular and set periods of study for the end results to be worthwhile.

The discipline needed for writing goes beyond filling a blank sheet of paper with words. You have to establish clearly in your own mind *what* you are attempting to achieve with your writing, and why. The same discipline applies to the construction of manuscripts, as well as the outline, synopsis, story-line, plot and research; even self-imposed deadlines are all part of the professionally attuned writer's craft. Make no mistake - very few folk are born with the natural ability to write really well. The disciplined writer has learned to recognise the recurring flaws in his/her work and is also able to realise when there is a need for a change of style or direction.

It doesn't matter what your working methods are (since we all work in different ways), or where and when you apply them - as long as a concerted effort is made to write a set number of pages every day/night. A literary agent once told me: "The road to any publisher's office is littered with dead MSS (manuscripts) of the 'one day I'll get down to it' brigade who failed to learn their craft, or come to terms with the professional attitudes required of today's successful author."

Lewis Hosegood:

"Discipline comes from regular work schedules on a weekly basis. We're all naturally inclined to be lazy. We find excuses to put off hard work - like mowing the lawn - and just dabble as the mood takes us. Since most writing classes have 'homework' or 'assignments', the deadlines, though scary, are good for us. Regularity is also important. Progress in ideas and techniques, like any other acquisition of skills, must be built up steadily. No one would expect a handyman to create a fine coffee table without hours of learning about mitre joints, gluing, sanding, finishing and polishing. The same applies to writing - whether it's an article, short story, novel or autobiography."

34

Writers' Block:

Which brings us, rather conveniently, to that over-milked excuse for not starting or completing a manuscript: Writers' Block! Does this condition really exist, or is it merely the amateur's grandiose plea for sympathy? A serious writer recognises the need for regular stimulation to generate ideas, followed by the dedication to transform those ideas into a well structured story or article. If the idea isn't working, and there isn't a dead-line to meet, leave it alone and do something else - read a book, do some gardening, take the dog for a walk or attend to the pile of research material that needs filing. When you eventually return to it a day, week or month later, you may just find the thing almost writes itself.

One *Quartos* reader commented: "I do seem to have a 'right' time for all my work, dictated by the project itself, rather than by me ... There always comes a point when I think 'that's enough for today'. If I ignore that and push on for another hour or so, those extra minutes usually yield the best stuff I've produced all day."

Lewis Hosegood:

"Yes, there certainly is such a condition as writer's block and the beginner should take comfort from the fact that we've all experienced it. For the novelist it's usually somewhere half way through the 'long distance run', or maybe earlier when the glorious enthusiasm of the opening has died down a little and you wake up wondering, 'What the hell now?'

With other forms of writing (short stories or poetry for example), it may be we go into a period of apparent non-inspiration. Terrifyingly, we tell ourselves we've 'dried up', lost touch. If we convince ourselves of this, we may indeed find it hard to get back. In fact it's unlikely that we have really dried up - we're more likely to be resting. Things are still going on inside. Just as in learning to swim, ride a bike, or drive a car, we seem to reach a plateau of progress. It's really consolidation. In a while we're making a great stride forward - and surprising ourselves!

What we have to do, with regard to writer's block, is not let it become an easy excuse for doing nothing. We must keep on writing. Something, anything which gives us pleasure. In the case of the novel we could leave things in abeyance and skip forward to some episode we've half envisaged and which we know we shall enjoy sketching out, even if we have to revise it later in the light of development. Or we could turn to something completely different - poetry, or a short story, or a bit of self-indulgent reminiscence - until inspiration returns. But we must not evade the issue, sooner or later we've got to work at it."

Nancy Smith:

"Writer's block does exist as most writers discover at some point in their career. There are many and varied suggested ways of dealing with it but its cause is probably due to lack of planning, so far as the novel is concerned, at least. Many novelists have experienced reaching chapters 3 or 4 and then getting stuck, not knowing where the story is going from there. They call it writer's block but it may be that the story-line isn't strong enough and needs to be abandoned, or it may be they should leave it for a while, and spend time thinking about both the plot and characters. Perhaps they should start on something else until enthusiasm is rekindled. Dead-lines are probably the most effective means of beating the dreaded blockage - they 'concentrate the mind wonderfully'. If a professional writer is commissioned to write a piece by a specific date, it's rare for them not to finish it by then."

Moe Sherrard-Smith:

"Writer's block! It isn't an infectious disease, the Dark Night of the Soul, nor something authors should expect to encounter: it should only be regarded as an occasional hiccough in the writing process. It's mildest - though most persistent - form is the reluctance to get started in the mornings. (Didn't Priestley say he'd sharpen his pencil for hours rather than write with it on the page?) That type of block is psychological, a kind of superstitious desire not to commit the idea to writing.

We hear a great deal today about 'wannabees'- including want-to-be writers. Here, I think, we have the 'maybees'. Maybe I won't get another idea? (So I'll treasure this one); Maybe I'll run out of steam? (So I'll keep on thinking for a while); Maybe I'll not be able to actually write at all? (And if I don't put words down, no one can criticise them).

If it's just a general 'can't write anything today' type of stoppage when words won't flow, then write something, anything, every day. Even if it's all to be thrown out, it doesn't matter. It just gets creativity flowing again and reinforces the writing habit. If it's a blockage with the current story or novel, it's often down to three things:

a) the synopsis isn't fully worked through, so the story-line's direction is uncertain;

or

b) the author doesn't know the characters well enough to know how they will react as the plot makes demands of them.

[With either of these reasons, it's advisable to take a few days to go back to the drawing board and check both plot and characterisation. Throw some unexpected problem in the character's path and see what twists and changes the story calls for as a result. The act of doing this can often get the author's reluctant subconscious kick-started. Alternatively, write something completely different, to divert the mind for a day or two]

or

(c) all the necessary research material isn't to hand. The answer is obvious, and the lack should be rectified.

Professional writers are less likely to be heard bemoaning writer's block because they recognise, by experience, the universal myth of the 'visiting Muse'. Yes, writing may be inspired, but it should be inspired by the *author's* dedication. That dedication has to come each day when the writing's in progress. How many novels would be written if the Muse had to be summoned and the author had to wait six months because she was on holiday? The fact is that virtually all novels are written by perspiration, not inspiration."

Postal Folios/Workshops:

An alternative to correspondence courses are the Postal Folios which operate around the UK. The folios work with a group of 6-8 writers of articles, poetry, novels or short stories, circulating manuscripts amongst themselves for criticism and advice from others members of the group.

The added advantage is that members are working with writers sympathetic to their own particular genre; this practice, however, still requires strict discipline as set dates are needed for posting so the folio is always in circulation. This method is ideal for anyone who is living in isolation or perhaps disabled, because it brings the work to your door while extending your circle of friends - polishing your writing skills at the same time. Postal folios are usually privately organised with several contacts listed in *The Writer's Handbook*.

Kate Dean is one of the organisers listed in the *WH* and also acts as liaison between other groups, to put interested novelists of the same genre in touch with each other: "There are scores of Manuscript Folios circulating throughout the country, providing criticism and market suggestions for writers of articles, short stories, poetry, etc. Many Folio members are unpublished when they first join and many owe their eventual publication to the help given by fellow members. Book Folios are for novelists and membership provides authors with up to five in-depth criticisms. As with Manuscript Folios, of course, there is no compulsion to follow the advice given, but often a suggestion will spark off an idea which can be incorporated in your re-write."

Unlike Manuscript Folios which circulate members' completed manuscripts together in one folder, the Book Folios circulate one chapter at a time and members receive one manuscript per week to read, criticise and post on to the next name on the rota. The most comprehensive listing of Postal Folios available in the UK is produced by Cathie Gill of Croftspun. *The Cottage Guide to Writers' Postal Workshops* gives the contact names and addresses and can be obtained from Drakemyre Croft, Cairnorrie, Methlick, Ellon, Aberdeenshire AB41 0JN.

Evening Classes:

Evening classes operating through local Education Authorities are highly recommended by Lewis Hosegood, although over the past couple of years there have been drastic cut-backs in adult education.

Lewis Hosegood:

"Here you may be sure the tutor is likely to be experienced and the course well structured. An obvious advantage over correspondence tuition is that you have instant personal contact - if you want advice you can get it on the spot. Classes have to be of a viable size - usually between 10 and 16 students - and will cost more than belonging to a local writers' group. The one I tutor charges £37 for a 12-week course (£27 for Senior Citizens). Attendance every week is not compulsory but obviously at that price you don't want to miss any!

Regular classes also provide stimulus. Ideas and challenges are constantly being offered which very often would not have occurred naturally to the student. One of my most successful short stories, *Homesickness*, broadcast four times on BBC, subsequently anthologized, and quoted in full in Nancy Smith's *The Fiction Writer's Handbook* came out of a title set as homework for a class I used to attend. I don't suppose for a moment I would have chosen it otherwise."

Writers' Circles:

Many writers find a great deal of support and encouragement in joining a local writers' group. These are usually made up of amateur writers, with a liberal sprinkling of successful authors in their midst. The circle can act as an effective sounding board for ideas and manuscript improvement, especially if you've had a few rejections and need a bit of friendly advice. It also gives writers the opportunity to widen their social circle and even those who go on to higher things, often maintain close ties with their original group. Although an established writer herself, Nancy Smith still enjoys the personal contact of her local writer's circle.

Nancy Smith:

"Writing is a lonely occupation and meeting others at whatever stage in their career provides vital stimulus. Also, everyone needs help at some point because we all have to learn the craft somehow. I certainly got my foot on the first step of my writing career through joining the Leicester Writers' Club due to the invaluable help I received there. Joining a writers' circle means you become part of that wonderful network of writers all over the country, meeting at conferences, seminars and so on, exchanging information and ideas in a supportive atmosphere. If there is a professionally- minded group near you, join it. If there isn't one, start one. You'll soon find others only too eager to belong."

Even writers' groups have their horror stories: as Editor of *Quartos*, I was invited to talk to a Circle and it had been suggested that I join them for the whole evening so that I could assess previously submitted manuscripts and make suggestions for improvement. Each member was also expected to read a piece of their own to give their fellows the opportunity to offer any constructive viewpoint. It quickly became obvious that newer members' work was provided as cannon fodder for the vitriolic remarks of the more 'experienced' members. The *piece de resistance* was so obscure that it had to be explained line by line, and finally given a rousing hum of approval because it had been penned by the Chairman's wife! I declined to participate.

Another of our readers wrote to tell us of his introduction to a local writers' group: "As an amateur scribbler and despite previous refusals, I was eventually press-ganged into attending a Circle meeting. I went along more out of courtesy than interest and attempted to join in the spirit of the thing by entering into a discussion. Having offered my four-penny-worth, I was treated to a scathing and insulting attack by the very person responsible for my being there. I realised that the reason for the prolonged silences during the evening were not due to lack of interest but because no-one else actually dared venture an opinion! The group was made up of extremely pleasant (and talented) people so why on earth did

40

they tolerate a mini-Hitler whom, I later discovered, was taking a postal writing course and flogging off copies of the lessons as though each one was his own idea? Needless to say I did not return."

If you join a Circle with which you are uncomfortable, don't be afraid to leave it and join another group. Like all 'groups' you need to find one that suits your personality, with people amongst whom you feel relaxed. If you don't feel that you belong, you will be resentful of the criticism and will gain nothing from the experience. There are bad groups, peppered with elitist smuggery, who use beginner's work as a punch-bag for their own malicious pleasure - I know, because I've given talks to them - but the majority are full of friendly, helpful people, so go out and find one that welcomes you.

Writers' Organisations:

For those interested in writing purely for fun, there is the **British Amateur Press Association**, whose 70+ members produce a collection of self-published pamphlets which they circulate among themselves. Founded over a hundred years ago, in 1890, the BAPA encourages members to contribute essays, stories and poems to existing publications, or to launch new ones of their own. This is not an outlet for commercial writing, but 'a fraternity providing contacts between amateur writers, journalists, artists, etc.'

A similar organisation operates as **The Society of Civil Service Authors**, which encourages the literary talents of past and present members of the Civil Service (and a wide range of others in the public utilities - for example, all members of the British Airports Authority, . N.H.S Nurses, Post Office and British Telecom are eligible.) The Society produces a lively bi-monthly magazine which acts as a focal point for the organisation with its numerous writing competitions, articles, letters, meetings and social events. Despite its title, members don't have to be an author to join.

Although not as well-known as it should be, **The University of the Third Age** offers retired people the opportunity to learn at their leisure, make new friends, and to take part in a wide variety of pastimes throughout the UK. Over the years they have built up an impressive U3A National Network for Creative Writing which arranges conferences and seminars for its members. The daytime meetings are informal and friendly, and most regional programmes appear to include a creative writing section amongst their numerous activities.

Writers' Workshops, Weekends & Courses:

In addition, there are hundreds of writing weekends, day workshops and courses taking place throughout the year all over Britain, catering for almost every aspect of creative writing. If you fancy a week or weekend amongst like-minded people, pick up a copy of the *Time To Learn* directory (published by NIACE, 19b De Montford Street, Leicester LE1 7GE).

As a result of government cut-backs many of the adult education courses are no longer available, however, it would be worth your while to check with your local college or arts centre to see if they are running a class. Apply to the Literary Officer at your local Regional Arts Board for inclusion on their mailing list so that you keep up-to-date with information on courses and workshops being organised in the area. A fee subsidy is often available for the unwaged or retired.

Although originally formed in London, the **Women Writers' Network** operated by Lyn Westerman offers reasonably priced workshops throughout the year. Currently celebrating their 10th anniversary, WWN began as a group of five freelance journalists and now has a national membership of over 300 working women journalists, poets, fiction and non-fiction writers. The Network is still London based but now has branches in both the North-East and North-West. The aim of the organisation is to help women writers further their professional development by providing a forum for the exchange of information, skills, support, career and networking opportunities.

The most famous of all writing courses are those held each year by **The Arvon Foundation**. Arvon is in fact three houses: Lumb Bank, an 18th century mill owner's house in West Yorkshire and

Totleigh Barton, a thatched manor house in North Devon and a new Scottish location. The atmosphere of an Arvon course is relaxed and designed to make students feel at home, since everyone contributes to the cooking and simple running of the house. The way each person spends their time is entirely up to them. There is the opportunity every day to discuss work with the tutors, while the evenings are usually devoted to informal readings of both the students' and tutors' work. No formal qualifications are needed and all that is asked of those taking part is, they have a genuine, active interest in writing. Those who have attended have nothing but praise for the instructional value of the tutoring.

A similar establishment has also been set up in Wales under **The Taliesin Trust**. Ty Newydd is an 18th century house in white-washed stone, some fifteen minutes walk from the sea. The courses provide the opportunity of working intimately and informally with two professional writers for four and a half days and offers a diverse programme of courses for all levels of writing throughout the year.

Another extremely popular event is the annual **Writers' Conference** held at the University of Southampton during April. This weekend is designed to help writers at all stages to learn the technical expertise of writing and publishing their work, by listening to lecturers on their own chosen area of writing. Delegates can attend seminars where the writer's previously submitted work is discussed by specialists, or bring along partial, completed or rejected manuscripts to workshops for revision under the guidance of published writers and publishers' representatives. An unique feature of the Conference are the 'Editor Appointments' which gives delegates the opportunity to discuss their manuscripts face to face with editorial representatives, who will help writers to understand how to successfully publish their work.

The Conference offers an extremely diverse programme of around 70 lectures and seminars, usually covering all aspects of writing, including plays for radio, television and theatre, poetry, the novel, writing for children's markets, literary and commercial short stories, feature writing, writing local history, biography and educational textbooks. There are also numerous workshops, writing competitions sponsored by various publishers, a book fair and the Civic Reception followed by the Writers' Dinner.

However for tuition on a more personalised level, the recommendations run high for the *How To Write A Novel* weekends with Moe Sherrard-Smith and Frederick Smith (author of the *633 Squadron* series). Nancy Smith has also spent many years as a correspondence school tutor before turning her talents to more personalised tutoring at venues such as Southampton University and Dillington.

Nancy Smith:
"The personal contact with students as on a residential week-end/ workshop/class is of great benefit to the students concerned. It means they can discuss in depth with the tutor any problems or difficulties they are experiencing in understanding any particular aspect of writing. They also gain from feedback from everyone else in the group. Thus, while correspondence courses may have their uses, especially for anyone house-bound, the advantages of attending a course of some kind are immense"

Cass Jackson:
"As a result of the popularity of our own Bournemouth weekends (now temporarily suspended) we founded the **FLAIR Network**, which is a sort of club for writers through which we can offer the support and advice often difficult to find elsewhere.

We've heard that people think they had to attend our writing weekends to be eligible for membership to the Network, but that's not true. Any writer, beginner or professional can join. Readers of our Newsletter so often asked for help with various problems, it seemed a good idea to enlarge our scope to include handbooks, cassettes, advisory and assessment services; we also have a Specialist Register through which members can make their own specialist knowledge available to other subscribers - and we cover a wide range of topics!"

Moe Sherrard Smith:
"Specialist workshops can offer a great deal, particularly from the point of an exchange of information and ideas with like minds - that is, others in tune with the creative process. Writing, whether of novels or short stories, can be divided into two parts: the 'craft', or mechanical techniques; and the 'art', that instinctive feel for story-telling and language. The former can be learned; writers must be born with the latter.

As my co-author and I lead many course and workshops on writing the novel, and I myself tutor by correspondence, we find the major benefit students derive is in learning to be totally objective about their own writing and in being fully aware that fiction does not just happen, it is created.

Of course, if criticism comes from a writer with a proven track record, or even from fellow students who are themselves 'writers', such criticism has a greater validity and is more acceptable than that from non-writers and friends anxious not to tread on delicate feelings."

Manuscript Assessment:

There's 'assessment' and then there's 'criticism'. Noel Coward ignored them; Robert Bolt was instructed by his mother not to play with them, Liberace cried all the way to the bank because of them. J. B. Priestley considered most to be parasites and Sibelius observed that no statue had ever been erected in tribute to one - and as a writer you'll discover dozens of 'em - CRITICS.

No one but a fool objects to *constructive* criticism and perhaps writers more than any other member of society, learn to glean more from a few well chosen and helpful words from an editor or publisher than any oratory from some self-appointed expert. Once, however, you have the confidence to say: "I am a writer," you become inundated with offers from all sorts of folk offering to read your work and tell you whether it's any good or not.

In her autobiography, Agatha Christie stated quite categorically that a writer should never give a manuscript to any member of the family to read. Half will tear it to shreds in their attempt to prepare you for the cruel reality of the rejection slip, while the other half will tell you how marvellous it is - regardless. There is heartache enough in professional rejection and criticism, so don't allow yourself to be persuaded by an overbearing relative into allowing them to read your work - give it to someone to assess professionally.

It may be that you've been submitting articles and short stories to countless publications and whilst the rejection slips are couched in polite terms, there is still something missing. It could be worthwhile to send a selection of your work to be assessed by a professional who can offer constructive help and advice for improvement. There may be some simple mistake that a few pounds worth of advice can rectify. Many new writers expect editors to offer advice on rejected manuscripts but believe me, very few editors have time to pen anything more than a handwritten line or two on a compliments slip - they are employed to acquire contributions for the magazine, not to act as unpaid writing tutors!

Nearly all writing magazines carry advertisements from individuals offering manuscript assessment. Unless a service states in which field the assessor has gained their experience, however, it is difficult to know whether they are going to be able to give a fair critique on your work. If the advertisement states they specialise in children's writing or romantic fiction, there is little point in sending off a 100,000 word block-buster on the Great War, without prior agreement. The majority of freelance assessors are usually willing to give an account of their writing experience, so make sure that the service you choose has the right background for reading your particular manuscript before paying any fees.

Possibly the most reasonably priced assessment services available are those offered by the Arts Councils or Regional Arts Boards under the auspices of their Literature Departments. Because all are government funded, the fees are affordable, even for a full length manuscript, although there have been drastic cutbacks due to the reductions in regional arts funding. RABs offering this service can call on all types of experienced writers living or working in the region to ensure that your manuscript is read by someone familiar with your particular genre.

The FLAIR Network offers 'Flair Comments' which give a completely honest opinion; if the work's good they'll say so, if it's not up to standard, they'll offer constructive ideas on how to improve it. In addition, the 'whole' script is edited. But perhaps the best recommendation for FLAIR Comments is that some clients who first approached them in 1988, still ask the Jackson's to vet their work, even though they've since become published writers. A top agent and two publishers also send clients to them from time to time.

The **Writers' Advice Centre** is a new development for Nancy Smith. Having started, and successfully run her own Fiction Critique Service for a number of years, she felt there was a need to widen its scope in some way. In order to do this, she teamed up with Jane Baker (an experienced journalist, short story writer and teacher of creative writing), and Louise Jordan (children's writer, reader for Puffin Books and ex-fiction editor of a teenage magazine). As a result, the Writers' Advice Centre is now in a position to offer sound, practical advice on all the important aspects involved in producing publishable writing. They cover adult fiction, long and short, as well as children's fiction, non-fiction and autobiography. They will also introduce authors to both publishers and agents where they feel the work is up to, or near to, publishable standard.

On a final note, be clear about what you expect from tutorial. Unless a course/workshop states that it is for beginners, the tutor is going to expect you to have some modicum of familiarity with what you are trying to achieve. The fact that you spend between two and four hours a day writing and have produced a 200,000 word novel would normally suggest that the writer has devoted some of that time to finding out about the publishing side of writing.

This is not always the case, as was demonstrated by a disgruntled workshop participant who complained to the organisers that she had been treated in a cavalier fashion by the tutor. Having submitted an extract which consisted of a complete Chapter 46 totalling a mere 1000 words, she was miffed because it was impossible to offer any sort of opinion or criticism as to its 'publishability'. This brief extract gave no indication of the author's ability to create a story, maintain a sense of action, develop characterisation, create atmosphere or hold a reader's attention. Having made the supreme effort in completing a full-length novel, any tutor would have expected her to understand that it's the *opening* that interests a publisher, not a 'filler' chapter three-quarters of the way through the manuscript.

The letter went on to ask why the tutor had not simply sent a request for the opening of the book since it had been submitted early enough for assessment. A publisher is *not* going to write and ask for the opening and if you've made the glaringly unprofessional mistake of sending Chapter 46 to titillate his interest, it's going straight in the bin. Harsh facts, perhaps, but publishers and tutors are not gurus, therapists, clairvoyants or miracle workers. You have to do most of the back-ground work yourself.

How-To Books:

Finally, we turn to the how-to books. There are hundreds available covering every aspect of creative writing but it is difficult to recommend those which will prove useful to your writing career and the ones to avoid. Be wary of the many American writing books that are on sale in the UK because often as not, they may not relate to writing for the British market. 'How-to' books should be looked on as a good investment and not purchased to be read once only - they need to be books you can refer to again and again throughout your career, no matter how experienced you become.

Publishers such as Allison & Busby, How-To Publications, A & C Black or Piatkus specialise in books on creative writing and it could be worth while to send for their current book list. However, always think twice before purchasing a how-to book on creative writing. Because the publisher needs to recover his initial outlay (and pay the author's royalties) the prices can be on the expensive side. It is very easy for the beginner to land up with a useless collection, so read the reviews in your chosen writers' magazine, make a note of the title, author and ISBN (the International Standard Book Number) and ask your library to order it for you.

This encourages the libraries to stock the books and the author gets paid a modest fee each time it is taken out.

PLR or Public Lending Right is calculated by a computerised sampling system which records the number of times a title is borrowed from certain public libraries, then multiplies the result. Approximately 2p per title borrowed is paid to the author each time his or her book is taken out of the library and, as all public libraries are bound to stock a title if asked for it, it makes sense to support your local library and ensure the author receives payment under the PLR scheme. This way *you* don't land up with a lot of unwanted how-to books with no re-saleable value.

Recommended Reading:

Updated annually, *The Writer's Handbook* edited by Barry Turner (Macmillan) gives full details of the Arts Councils and Regional Arts Boards, and a wide selection of independent postal folios, festivals, writers' courses, circles and workshops. All the key markets are covered including publishers, packagers, poetry outlets, magazines, newspapers, TV, radio, theatre and video companies, together with writing related articles on agents, tax and the small presses.

The Writers' & Artists' Yearbook is published annually by A & C Black. Every writer should possess a copy of the current edition, since this is one reference book that should be renewed each year. Although covering an immense range of publications, agents and publishers, there is only enough room to provide limited information about each. Nevertheless, an invaluable overall reference book.

Chapter 3   Research & The Market Place

Why do writers receive rejection slips? From an Editor's point of view, my answer would be because very few bother to perfect the technique of sound market research and their submissions work very much on a hit-or-miss basis. Even more experienced writers attending literary workshops reveal a noticeable lack of knowledge and application when it comes down to identifying their own individual market outlets.

When you begin your writing career, the most vital lesson you should learn is the importance of thoroughly researching the marketplace for potential outlets. This is not merely a question of sending along something in similar vein hoping for an acceptance; it is the continual study of a particular publication so you become familiar with the editor's preferences. Once you have mastered the formula, all should be plain sailing - until a new editor is appointed and you have to begin all over again. Whatever the publication, there is no short cut to success and no substitute for sound market research.

It doesn't matter how competent you are with the written word, it will be of no avail if you haven't concentrated your efforts on finding out all there is to know about your target magazine(s). Whether you are writing a short story, novel or magazine article, you must know BEFORE you start, where you intend to submit the finished manuscript.

Your first job is to read as many newly published works written within your own genre: study the short stories and articles appearing in the magazines you wish to write for; find out who is publishing novels in your chosen field; who likes your kind of poetry.   Make a note of the features which distinguish those successful submissions - only then may you hope to emulate or surpass them.

One agent told us: "Become a sleuth' and you will eventually solve the problem of breaking the market barrier." These barriers *do* exist and if you intend to be successful in your marketing approach, you need to recognise this fact.   You may be totally familiar with your own manuscripts and writing style but how familiar are you with the vagaries of the editor/publishing house?

Make it your business to learn, because it is not enough these days just to be able to write. To push yourself ahead in the competitive field of freelance writing, you will need to familiarise yourself with the functions of an editor (presentation and originality); the market researcher (supply and demand, i.e.. the publisher AND the reader); the salesman (placing your manuscript before the right buyer) and even the financial controller (budgeting your own account)!'

Knowing Where To Look:

The majority of magazines accepting freelance contributions are more than pleased to provide a set of writer's guidelines for interested writers on receipt of a stamped addressed envelope, although they (and most creative writing tutors) will recommend you study at least 25 stories or articles from a particular magazine before submitting work for consideration.

Question: How do you discover which particular editorial require-ments provide the key to each individual magazine?

Answer: By selecting half a dozen copies of a magazine in which you would like to be published and studying it meticulously.

Often writing tutorials suggest a visit to your local newsagent or library will suffice; however, a visit to your high street charity shop or local jumble sale will usually provide you with a better selection of reduced price copies which you can take home and study at your leisure. Leaving the library and newsagents until you have developed a more experienced eye for snap market analysis.

Choose the most current issues available and read through each magazine very carefully, paying particular attention to the advertisements because these give an even clearer indication of the age/reader/market profile for that particular publication. If you intend to submit short stories, you will need to analyse the plots of those already published to ascertain whether the editor prefers romance, crime, twist-in-the-tale, humour or other themes; are the fictional characters young, middle aged or retired? What sort of the background, occupation or interests do the stories reflect?

Magazines are filled with all sorts of articles, on a vast variety of subjects but again you will need to analyse a selection of those already accepted by the editor before submitting anything of your own. What sort of style appeals to the readers? Are the examples factual, argumentative, emotive, how-to? Do they offer a subject for discussion, or do they merely mirror the author's opinion? From the six magazines you have chosen for analysis, pick three articles from each and compare them with the following:

a) Do the majority of articles contain any new ideas, or ideas linked with current news or issues?

b) If the article covers a familiar subject, is it written from a fresh and interesting angle? If so, outline the point of interest.

c) Does the title catch the eye, and if so, why?

d) Does the lead paragraph hold your attention and is the subject clearly introduced in the opening paragraph?

e) Does the article have a surprise ending and is the ending linked to the title and opening paragraph?

f) Do the articles consist of long or short paragraphs? Do long or short words predominate? How many words to a sentence? Does the article comprise of easy to understand words?

g) Is the house-style of the publication chatty, friendly, formal or pompous?

h) At what type of person are the advertisements aimed?

Preparing the foundations for any type of work can be boring, so we asked our writing tutors if they had any favourite tips for making market research interesting or easier:

Cass Jackson:
"The answer to this has to be mercenary. The most interesting part of market research is how much money you can expect to earn if your offering is accepted. Bluntly, if a writer can't be bothered to spend time researching a market for her work, she is obviously not much concerned about getting published."

Moe Sherrard-Smith:
"This is a vitally important area which is often dismissed by amateurs as irrelevant and (in their own individual case) unnecessary. The only way to make research interesting, is to actually *want* to do it. If you're enthused by the subject, you'll attack research with that much more vigour and interest. After all, it isn't researching 'dead' facts, but snippets of information, gossip, scandal, whatever."

Lewis Hosegood:
"The writer must certainly study the market carefully over a period of time (preferably not just one issue). Another tip I would offer, with consumer magazines especially, is to study the advertisements. These often set the tone, age range and outlook of the journal very clearly. After all, the magazine probably depends upon its advertisers for existence, so in a way they're a form of sponsorship. So a glossy that has a lot of adverts for alcohol, cigarettes, fast cars, expensive holidays abroad, will probably not take kindly to an elderly, preachy article about the good old days. An informed one about AIDS might be better received."

Nancy Smith:
"Regularly spend an hour or so browsing along magazine racks in large newsagents. When you find one or two which interest you, buy at least three issues to study in more depth. Spend any waiting

time at the doctor's or dentist's surgery, or at your hairdresser's, profitably, by looking at any magazines left out."

The Dreaded Word Count:

Another reason why it is best to obtain copies of your potential outlet for home study is explained by well-known writing tutor and former Editor of *Writing* magazine, Barbara Horsfall, when it comes down to the next valuable exercise - the word count.

"In order to get you started, count across a full line of the paragraph. Pencil the total down in the right margin. Now count how many lines down make 100. Pencil that in the right margin and always pencil in the total of words written at the bottom of each page. This is the bane and necessity of all writers' lives. So start now; it is a habit that must become second nature. Of course, you're wondering why?

The reason is that an editor's space and layout is of prime importance, with particular needs for each magazine. Long before your manuscript arrives for perusal, space has already been allocated. So the editor glances at your title, checks whether it is an article or short story, and immediately looks to see whether the length (the word count YOU have provided) will fit in. On rare occasions, if a piece of work is extremely good, but over the required length, it may be retained for a future issue of the magazine and space will be made for it. Otherwise your script will come winging back with a rejection slip - not because there's anything wrong with the content, but simply because no editor has the time to sit and count words of work forwarded to them. This is ALWAYS the author's job."

Getting To Know The Editor:

One aspect of editorial policy is almost impossible to detect, unless you have insider-information and this is the subject of an editor's prejudices. One regular *Quartos* contributor raised the question on discovering one lady editor's refusal to accept anything bearing a man's name; another was alleged to detest anything referring to Wales! As Alexander Fullerton observed in *The*

Publisher: "Editors have blind spots - no editorial judgement can ever be 100% objective." It is an interesting point and probably the majority of editors do have pet hates when it comes to subject and/or a particular writing style.

I confess to a loathing of short stories composed *entirely* of dialogue, mawkish sentimentality over animals and anything with 'Mummy' in the first sentence. I personally know of an editor of a general interest women's magazine who will not publish anything that is even *remotely* connected to New Age thinking - even herbal remedies, astrology and superstition get the thumbs down. Yet another reader found out (too late) that he'd sent a piece on a local Master of Foxhounds to an editor who abhorred blood sports. Unfortunately, the only way you will ever discover individual editorial quirks is via grapevine gossip but they do exist.

I recently received a telephone call from a new-comer to freelance writing, who offered to sell book reviews to *Quartos* for a substantial fee of £50.00 each Having explained that we were only interested in writing-related book reviews, but would possibly consider fiction reviews on books by new writers, providing they were coupled with publisher's comments of why those authors had been added to their particular publishing list, our freelancer confessed that she would be unable to produce the 'goods'. Her aim had been to sell the same book review to a series of different magazines but did not have the contacts, or the ability to produce what was asked of her. The whole secret of market research is *being able to supply an editor with what s/he wants, not what you want to write.*

Market Sources & Reference:

There are several publications which provide brief background details of magazines and publishers which could be considered as possible outlets for your work. It is important to understand, however, that the brief details given in the handbooks and directories *are insufficient as guides in themselves.* You will still need to study a few recent back issues to get the full flavour of the magazine before submitting your manuscript.

The three major publications are *The Writers' & Artists' Yearbook,* *The Writers' Handbook* and *Willing's Press Guide.* All are up-dated annually but the cost of *Willing's* is prohibitive, so most of us have to make do with the municipal copy at the local library. This publication is the most comprehensive guide to the newspaper and periodical industry in the UK and abroad, listing 3,700 newspapers, 15,600 periodicals and 2,500 annuals worldwide.

The Magazine Writer's Handbook by Gordon Wells (Allison & Busby) and *1000 Markets for Freelance Writers* by Robert Palmer (Piatkus) cover most of the established national magazines, including guide-lines for fiction and non-fiction, circulation figures, how to approach the editor, payment, etc.

No such publication exists for the hundreds of small press publications which usually provide the vital first acceptances for the beginner. The most comprehensive directory to small press publishing (see Chapter 9) is the *Small Presses & Little Magazines of the UK & Ireland* published by Oriel Bookshop, but this does not give any indication of the *type* of material accepted by each individual publication. Quarterly *Zene Magazine* is new on the market but it also provides up-to-date information on the independent publishers of the small press. Nevertheless, there are always promises of new small press directories and the only way you will find out about them is through a subscription to a regular writers' magazine.

Whilst not a visually impressive publication for the price, *Free-lance Market News* contain valuable information on both UK and foreign markets. Published monthly for over 25 years, every issue of *FMN* contains around 60 different editorial requirements for national and small press publications. For a monthly guide to new magazines, defunct publications, competitions, changes of editorial policy, marketing tips, overseas outlets, etc., *FMN* can be an extremely good investment.

There are other outlets for freelance writing which are not always considered by the beginner, and if you have any specialist knowledge of a particular trade, profession or hobby, there is usually a magazine or newsletter catering for those with similar interests. The trade publications offer quite substantial fees for articles accepted and should not be overlooked. A popular small press publication covering this aspect of freelance writing is Geoff Carroll's *Writers' Guide,* which also produces a regular guide to short story outlets and other market-place information.

Don't ignore local newspapers and 'free' papers which regularly use short articles because they also provide an outlet for freelance writers. Several *Quartos* readers have a regular column in local 'free' papers and have learned a great deal from the experience since they still require discipline to produce ideas on a regular basis. Last but not least, never overlook local and national radio and television companies as outlets for drama/short stories/interviews/news features, etc.

Market Research and the Full-length Book:

Effective market research is not only applicable to submitting articles and short fiction to magazines - the same rules apply to writers undertaking any full-length work. It doesn't matter whether your book is fiction or non-fiction, for adults or children, you still need to spend a considerable amount of time finding out which publishers favour your particular kind of writing. Find out whether manuscripts are restricted to a maximum of 80,000 words, or less; or whether the publishers prefer much longer works.

Read as many books currently published in your chosen genre and try to plot the subtle shift in market trends; bear in mind that publishers are now beginning to put out first editions in paper-back, which cost less to produce than hardback. From an author's point of view, *The Writer's Handbook* is the best place to start because this gives an up-to-date (but not infallible), outline of the type of manuscripts publishers are willing (or unwilling) to consider. A couple of hours in the public library will also show you which publishing houses have been accepting the type of material you are trying to write. Modern imprints carry details of the book's printing history after the title page and will tell you when the book was published.

Publishers' catalogues also provide in-depth information as to what is currently being marketed by the publishing industry. Usually issued twice a year, ask your local bookshop for any unwanted catalogues giving details of the latest titles. Do bear in mind, though, that the contracts for these *new* titles were probably signed some 18 months to two years previously and the publisher may have had a change of policy since then.

Background Research:

The other side of the informational coin is the research needed to give added depth to both fiction and non-fiction. Market research for possible outlets is a necessary chore but *background* research can become an addictive practice. All too many writers re-hash tired old reference sources rather than delve into archives to produce some fascinating new tit-bit of information to stimulate reader interest. Any form of writing needs 'atmosphere' and it is this attention to detail that can make writing come alive. Even the simplest of plots requires a degree of background authenticity to give the whole thing reader appeal.

Nancy Smith:

"... But you must be accurate. If you aren't thoroughly familiar with the background you're writing about, make sure you undertake the necessary research."

Lewis Hosegood:

"Do you know that your local librarian will probably be glad to help with research? With so much information on computer, a librarian can get through to the County Library at the touch of a button. Don't be afraid to ask, it's surprising how many people love to think they're helping an actual author! Some years ago, needing background information for a novel set in an Italian palazzo, I wrote to the tourist office in Vicenza. I received loads of marvellous stuff (in English), including historical details, brochures and pictures that I was able to use descriptively. The gallant gentleman finished by wishing me well with the book."

Moe Sherrard-Smith:

"If you can, visit the places important to the book, to soak up the atmosphere, even though significant details may have to be changed over the years.   Where possible, interview people who have connections with the places or events - most are happy to talk about such things. The excitement interviews generate is contagious, and one question leads to another ... But beware, research can become addictive, and the book (or article) may never get written. What   any form of research *should* do is boost the author's confidence that the work will be accurate in detail and /or period flavour."

Lewis Hosegood:

"What I think is important is the use to which you finally put this knowledge.   The author needs to know more than s/he relates. Beginners (in historical fiction especially) seem to think they have to use absolutely everything.   This makes for tedium when the average reader just wants to get on with the story.   Just one striking reference to a common place of the day (like the sound of iron-rimmed carriage wheels on flints) is worth more than a long dissertation on the state of the state of the roads before John McAdam.

As for style, I'd recommend writers to steep themselves in the literature of the period (the Regency, say) whether it's Jane Austen, Thackeray, Georgette Heyer or the 'Hornblower' series of C. S. Forester, they'll then produce a language which is neither fustian nor jarringly modern."

This advice doesn't only apply to historical novels; any form of plot whether it be wartime, foreign location, occult, science fiction, espionage, etc. needs time spent researching the period or place.   Since most women's epic fiction traces the main character's climb from rags to riches, it is essential for the author to be familiar with war-torn Paris, New York during the depression, Edwardian London, or Australia's penal colonies, to give the story added zest. The more efficient your attempts at researching your markets and backgrounds, the less chance you have of your work disappearing into a bottomless pit of unsuitable manuscripts.

Moe Sherrard-Smith:

"For fiction, the research may be just as vital, but will possibly never feature in the novel, other than by passing reference. That is, because research is *background, not content.* Use it sparingly in a novel, bearing in mind that all details ought to be essential to the plot and move the story-line along. Long catalogues of descriptive details leave readers with the distinct impression that buying a guide-book would have been a better proposition."

Lewis Hosegood:

"The same care needs to be taken with geographical research. If you're setting your tale in, say, Vienna, you need to know every park and square and monument like the back of your hand. (You don't need to go there; a street plan will do). But you don't need to drag it all in - a little touch of local colour is often enough. In a novel I recently finished, I wanted to describe Hitler's triumphal entry into Vienna during the Anschluss of 1938. I wasn't there so I don't know, but from research I could work out his route, the number of vehicles of his entourage, etc. And because it was April, I guessed the daffodils would have been out in the Rathaus Park where I planted my observer, hoping that this small detail would help bring it alive.

Another gimmick I've found useful is to have a hanging calendar as 'Observation Notes'. Make a brief reminder whenever appropriate, such as Oct 18 .. 'bracken turning colour'. Then you won't have it too early, or too late, in some tale you're writing next April. Nor will you make the mistake of describing apple, plum, cherry and horse-chestnut blossom all out at the same time!"

Cass Jackson:

"Research is very important, whatever you're writing. Even if you're only writing a 1000 word short story, set in the present, it's vital to check the details - for example, what is the number of the bus which runs in the area you mention, what colour is it, how often does it run, and so on. Whether you're writing fiction or non-fiction, it's a good rule to check everything that can be checked. Editors don't like it when readers point out writers' mistakes."

Lewis Hosegood:

"For non-fiction, research is essential. I can't think of any subject where the writer has sufficient personal knowledge to write a book on it, except perhaps autobiography - and even there you would need to check dates, places, local events, etc. surely? If you were just writing a gardening article, wouldn't you want to check other articles, books and your own notes? Facts are so important."

Moe Sherrard-Smith:

"Research for a non-fiction book is paramount, since it will form the essential background scaffolding around which the book is constructed. Above all, it has to be accurate and, in non-fiction works, must be given due credit by footnotes and/or bibliography. Plagiarism is passing off someone else's work as your own. Whilst researching, therefore, keep meticulous notes of sources and quotations."

Nancy Smith:

"With fiction it depends on the type, of course. An historical novel (even a historical romance) would certainly need some background research. Science fiction, if it's not to be all gobbledegook, needs some technical knowledge for plausibility. Fantasy is all the better for an awareness of the Greek and Arthurian legends. And so on. 'Straight' or mainstream fiction has more latitude. Some people say they don't need any research for their type of writing, it's tedious and time-consuming. It all comes out of their imagination. But surely we all need to check things from time to time? Even if it's only a quotation. (Especially if it's a quotation!) Or maybe the date of a pop song, film, or who was the U.S. President in 1975? I know my desk-side reference books are all in constant use."

Discussing the problems of making historical novels come alive, another of our contributors posed the question: "Have you ever considered removing your knickers and, clad in two metres of old sheet as a sole undergarment, augmented with a blanket petticoat and shawl - creeping outside at earliest dawn to gather enough twigs and garden rubbish to build a small sullen fire to heat the breakfast porridge pot?"

or

"Consider tying a metal bar some three and a half feet long and weighing four to six pounds on one hip, balancing it with a similar 18" length on the other. Now try running up a steep spiral stair with uneven treads and in partial darkness to test the truth behind: 'Armed with sword and dagger, he ran up to the battlements'."

Almost every aspect of history, sport, art, literature, industry or craft has its own Society or Guild who will readily provide background material or advice on the best sources for your research. As Barbara Horsfall pointed out in an article: "Whatever setting you're using, be sure you know enough about it to write with a degree of authenticity. In other words, write about what you know - or take the trouble to find out. A few library books will soon enable you to take enough notes to portray seemingly factual surroundings or skills. It may be a craft centre, an office setting, cabinet making, or even a place abroad. If it's the latter and you've never been there, a delve into everything you can find out about it is a must. Whatever setting or skill you choose, remember that although you've not worked at cabinet making, or been abroad to your chosen spot, you can bank on at least one of your readers who has. So don't bluff, research instead."

One instance that springs to mind which aptly demonstrates the need for researching a subject was an historical romance that included only a handful of words to give a medieval flavour. Back in the good old days of publishing this 200 page novel had been accepted despite the fact that there were only 98 'period' words in the entire text that was supposed to reflect a Plantagenet background - I counted them. Apart from the odd smattering of 'doublet', 'hose', 'dungeon', 'banqueting-hall', 'portcullis', etc., there wasn't one authentic historical paragraph to set the scene. A similar manuscript would be instantly rejected in the 1990s for lack of convincing detail, because today's reader expect more from a novel.

Similarly there are basic scientific laws governing science fiction which are ignored at your peril. As another of our contributors pointed out: "Laws of science apply everywhere you go; in space, on another planet, or on post-holocaust Earth. Laws of gravity, of genetics, whatever you want to discuss. You might decide to take refuge in the old Sword & Sorcery fantasy world, where magic can rule supreme, but even magic has its own laws!"

Original Thought:

Research does not necessarily end with the collecting of ideas through reading. To add a professional dimension to features and full-length books, you will need to interview people who have experience of your subject. Editors and publishers want original material which includes input from fresh sources; it is not enough to regurgitate previously published ideas, you need to think of some new ones of your own. Which brings us to the third key-word after *Information* and *Discipline - Originality*.

Lewis Hosegood:

"Hints for sparking off an original idea? I wish I knew! But I would recommend non-fiction writers to look critically through magazines and library shelves to try and find a subject that doesn't seem to have been touched upon before. Or alternatively, treat a popular subject from an entirely different angle. Animal Welfare may be 'in' so why not have a chat with your friendly vet and get some information on the relative value of dog biscuits against bones? There's no law against using other people's ideas but avoid re-hashes, and especially vague generalisation."

Moe Sherrard-Smith:

"To spark off ideas, the best advice is to open up the imagination to possibilities in the most unlikely places. A snatch of conversation overheard on a bus; an agony aunt letter; someone else's life story. But all the time remember that one idea isn't sufficient for a novel; without embellishment and dramatic re-arrangement, no-one's life is fully a book. In *Write A Successful Novel*, we give a prime example of how a small newspaper item sparked a host of possibilities for the construction of a plot. Taking a snippet of information and bombarding it with 'what if?' questions is a marvellous way to get going."

Nancy Smith:

"Eavesdropping in cafes, buses or other public places can often spark off ideas for short stories. Or take the opening line of a published story and go on from there."

It is not easy to be original - after all, even the philosophers tell us that there's no such thing as original thought. As far as writing is concerned, being original means trying to find a different *approach* to a subject, to portray it from another angle, play devil's advocate and offer an alternative viewpoint in both your fact and fiction. Having set a 'flower' theme for a *Quartos* reader's fiction competition, I added the suggestions that it could be a funerary tribute, a stone carving on an ancient tomb or a dried blossom pressed between the pages of a book. The result - half the entries were about a rose and quite a large number were actually titled *The Rose!*

At most *Quartos* writers' workshops, I demonstrate the lack of spontaneous originality by this simple exercise of word association:

"I'm going to give you one simple word and want you to write the first thing that comes into your head. Don't think about it, just write it. This isn't a trick to make you seem foolish, so don't try to be clever. The first thing you think of ... Water."

The majority of answers are usually common-place things like tap, glass, stream, rain, etc., but the second time around, when they've had time to think about it and see how mundane and repetitive their responses were, we generally come up with answers which are visually poetic. By the time we've gone through earth, fire and air, they've really got the hang of *not* writing about the first thing that comes to mind. It's a simple exercise but an effective one for demonstrating just how trivial first thoughts can be.

Using Original Source Material:

Writer Gal Travers hit the nail squarely on the head when it comes to tackling in-depth research which takes you out into the community. "The truth of course, is that one writes a book on a subject because one *does know* what one is talking about. There's little point in attempting to write from a position of ignorance, but even if you do know something about the field you've chosen, there's no doubt that it will require further research - and if it's a controversial or sensitive topic this is where your difficulties begin.

If you are dealing with human experience, how do you get the subjects you need to talk to, to trust you enough to be open and honest? A reputation for honesty helps but if you're working in the field of journalism, simply mentioning the job description 'journalist' may raise a sneer of contempt. So, having begun researching and writing a book (also a series of feature-length articles) on a facet of gay male life, I discovered that gay men often live in secrecy through fear of the opinion of others. Finding and contacting them is, in itself, a task which requires tact, contacts and a degree of doggedness."

A fellow writer researching the intricacies of occult practice in the UK found a similar problem, but original material was necessary for the book, so the author was forced to persevere. "It took a long time to gain the confidence of the people I wanted to talk to, but I kept hammering away until I was given access to the most amazing archive on witchcraft from 'within the circle'. These contacts led to others, here in Britain and the States, but I couldn't have reached them without personal introductions and a tremendous amount of personal trust. They had little enough reason to trust a journalist but I'd researched my subject well before I'd attempted to make contact, and was able to convince some important people of my sincerity in giving them a fair hearing."

What To Do With It When You've Found It:

Good research also demands an effective and efficient filing system to house the material collected. Check every publication that comes your way and retain everything which might have a use at some future date. A series of coloured plastic folders or A4 manila envelopes and a sturdy cardboard storage box should suffice since these can be stored neatly away until required. Up-to-date material can always be worked into topical articles and shows that you are keeping abreast with the latest developments in your chosen specialist area. Which methods do our contributors favour when it comes to storing all those clippings, research notes, background information, etc?

Cass Jackson:

"We differ here. Janie uses the 'deep litter' system. Keep everything in a pile: when you want to find something, throw it all in the air and snatch at the sheets as they descend! A good memory is also an asset. I rely on clearly labelled folders, kept in alphabetical order, in a filing cabinet. This system has the merit of being practically fool-proof, in that the alphabetical sequence makes it almost impossible to lose anything. A file is opened for each book, and inside that file I keep clearly labelled envelopes.

For example - I want information about the venue in which my novel *The Red Chrysanthemum* is set. I go to the file marked *The Red Chrysanthemum* and look in the envelope marked 'Venues'. Elaborate cross referencing and similar systems can take up an awful lot of time which could be better spent in actually writing."

Lewis Hosegood:

"Whether market or just background research, organise some convenient system of ready tabulation. This can take any preferred form - notebook, card filing system, word processor disk, etc. Work out in advance a series of suitable headings for your requirements.

For me as a novelist it might be: Dates ... Places ... Relationships ... Events ...Things To Do ... etc. but for an article writer is could be:

Market ... Preferred Length ... Sub-Heads? ... Illustrations ... Date Sent ... Returned ... Remarks ... etc., Then as you come up with observations you can jot them in.

Clippings go in a document wallet file with dividers and having recently acquired a word processor, I find it convenient to keep some information on a separate floppy disk under different file headings such as those already mentioned. Probably quicker to refer to is a simple filing system of postcards in a cardboard box - you just flick through them.

Collecting picture postcards is also an excellent idea. Recently holidaying in Austria I picked up a card of Hitler's 'Eagle's Nest' conference room at Berchtesgaden as it was in his day (it's now a restaurant). There is was - shape of the room, furniture, carpet, wall-decoration, everything! As it happened, I didn't need to use any of it - but *knowing* the atmosphere gave me, I felt, the confidence to write better. Which brings me back to my point: always research more than you use."

Moe Sherrard-Smith:

"My own research material is divided into two systems. Clippings, photographs, etc., occupy a large number of filing boxes, sorted under different categories - often with cross references. My early written notes were treated under the same system. Nowadays, particularly with notes culled from books, radio and TV documentaries and interviews, such information is kept on computer database. This does allow a good and fast searching facility without disturbing the accumulated dust on old boxes!"

Nancy Smith:

"Large, sturdy, used envelopes are a cheap and effective method of filing away clippings, etc."

As well as collecting market-place/research information, you need to give some thought to establishing personal files in which you keep snippets, cuttings, brochures, etc., for future reference and article ideas. This is where those out-of-date editions of *Pear's*

Cyclopedia can come in useful. However, it is equally important not to disappear under a mounting collection of files, boxes and envelopes stuffed with paper.

Another reader warned that it was just as important to be discerning about what you *discard*. Have a few markets in view that you are trying to sell manuscripts to, and pick out the kind of ideas that will appeal to them; if possible, make your subjects topics that bring you pleasure and which you already know something about.

Although it is inadvisable to become bogged down with out-dated books and cuttings, I would advise extreme caution in disposing of material too hastily - especially if your subject is historical or political. We have seen recently how smear campaigns and media-mongering have altered the face of current affairs. What appears to be up-to-date news today may be tomorrow's smoke-screen, and adding back-dated controversial comparisons to your non-fiction (or fiction) may make all the difference to the commissioning editor or publisher.

Likewise, history books that have been proved to be sheer bunkum still have their uses - because very often the sources were used as school text books! Conflicting opinions are also a must if you want to add spice to your article, and even if you think that Richard III really was responsible for the murders in the Tower, most editors would now expect you to mention both sides of the argument to forestall any pot-shots from members of The White Boar Society! Therefore, you will need reference books/clippings supporting opposing opinions to demonstrate that you have fully researched your piece. If your interest is history and/or politics, be sure that what you are about to discard really has no life left in it - or you may regret it.

A Question of Payment:

Although *Quartos* began life as a 12 page competition news-letter, it was decided right from the start, a token payment would be offered for any full length articles accepted for publication. There is an unfortunate, but true, sales adage that states that 'anything costing nothing, is worth nothing,' and I wanted contributors to feel that their work was worth paying for, however humble the fee. It's a personal choice, however, and if you're willing to have work accepted without payment (and since the majority of small press publications only pay in complimentary copies), then no one can say you are wrong.

In a 'Letter to the Editor' one reader upheld the view that whilst writers who are trying to establish themselves are usually very happy just to have work accepted and see their name in print, when it comes to *continued* acceptances it raises the question: "Well, if they like it then it's worth something and should be paid for, surely?" Our reader quite rightly believed that all writers eventually expect to receive payment for what they produce and once the first flush of pleasure at seeing your work in print has passed, you may well decide that from now on you will only write for a fee. But how do you decide?

Graham Stevenson:

"Few freelance writers earn sufficient from their pen to make a living. Most have other incomes - often from unrelated jobs. Fishmonger by day, penman by night. Does this matter? Different people write for different reasons, the thought of money is seldom one of them. For many, writing and being published for its own sake is motive enough.

Very often, the beginner is advised to aim low. If you target smaller, less well-known markets, your chances of an acceptance will be greater than if you aim at the national glossies. The pickings may not be rich but at least you'll get published. I've often said beginners should target lower markets to help them win acceptances.

Financial reward should take second place. Until, that is, work begins to sell on a regular basis. A few years ago, I reached the stage where I was selling 95% of my work. The trouble was, I wasn't exactly getting wealthy - I'd sold a lot, but not for a lot. I decided then, to aim higher in some of my writing whilst continuing to target my more usual outlets and while my acceptance rate fell to some extent, my income rose considerably.

Once you begin to sell regularly you need a grim determination to raise your sights to greater things. The statistics surrounding freelance writers who make a living from it are not encouraging. One publisher has estimated that "less than 1% of manuscripts from any publisher's slush pile ever sees publication." *Bella's* Fiction Editor, Linda O'Byrne, has said she receives around 800 unsolicited manuscripts every month. How many does she accept? She says: "I'm lucky if I find one in three months." One in 2,400 is hardly good odds.

The freelancer who writes for the joy of it has two choices: either he sticks to those markets he can conquer with little thought of financial reward, or he can push harder and harder until one day he makes the big time. Admittedly, the gap between the small press and the glossies can seem impossibly wide; how many well-known authors ever thought they would become well-known when they first set pen to paper? Many started small and expanded as they gained experience. So, perhaps, should you. Once you've seen a degree of success, you too can afford to be bolder and go for the money. Just how bold should you be?

In the end it is up to the individual what s/he accepts in payment. For the hungry writer though, a fee acceptable at the beginning of a writing career will fail to inspire later on. Against this, I still write for little financial reward when I have a sympathy for the cause of the publication concerned. Some magazines are worthy of support irrespective of their rates of pay but in the main I earn between £20 and £100 per thousand words because market forces say that is the going rate. This is infinitely better for my bank balance than the level of fees I earned a few years ago.

So far as the aspiring freelance is concerned, the principle is simple: begin small and success will follow. Move up one rung of the ladder at a time and almost without you noticing it, your output will become good enough to command a decent rate for the job."

Recommended Reading:

1000 Markets For Freelance Writers by Robert Palmer (Piatkus) is an A-Z guide to general and specialist magazines and journals, and a very good reference source for possible outlets because it is geared specifically towards the demands of the typical freelance writer. ISBN: 0-7499-1288-X

The Magazine Writer's Handbook by Gordon Wells (Allison & Busby) is up-dated every couple of years and is an indispensable guide for all freelance writers, providing detailed information on over seventy British magazines - and comments on many more. Each magazine has a page devoted to the type of articles and short stories normally considered by the editor, with an outline of the acceptable wordage.

An invaluable addition to anyone's library shelf, *Research for Writers* by Ann Hoffman (A&C Black). The revised and expanded edition includes organisation and methods of research; sources of information and their location; factual and historical research; research for fiction writers, dramatists, biography, family and local history. Plus some of the pitfalls to be avoided by the 'novice' researcher, and the particular problems facing writers of fiction and non-fiction. ISBN: 0-7136 3584-3

Chapter 4   The Right Approach

"DON'T WASTE MY TIME!" How would you feel if your manuscript came back with these words scrawled across the rejection slip ... hurt ... offended? Every day hundreds of writers waste the time of editors, agents and publishers because they insist on ignoring the basis rules of presentation and approach. We have seen how important it is to send material to the right place, but there is also a right and wrong way to submit the finished manuscript.

According to a recent MORI poll: "Britain is a nation of secret and would-be authors in which one in 50 of the population claims to have written a book and three in 10 believe they have a book in them." Nevertheless a report in *The Daily Telegraph* indicates that the figures have not surprised The Publisher's Association. "Most of the books written in this country do not get published because they are not good enough ... There's certainly been an increase in books written and published because self-publishing is much easier that it used to be. But many of them are terrible ..."

The writer is a peculiar breed of animal when it comes down to presenting his finished manuscript for consideration. He will spend weeks or several years creating a work that he hopes will eventually appear on the shelves of the local bookshop, but devotes little time to the presentation of his creation. Once the manuscript has left his possession, however, it is beyond his control and will stand or fall on its own merits.

Whilst a beautifully presented manuscript will not guarantee success, a pristine copy, clearly typed will at least catch the reader's eye. Make no mistake, the appearance of a manuscript can make all the difference between it being picked up, and read, or discarded unread because its presentation is poor.

One agency told us that they consistently receive manuscripts which fail to meet the most basic of presentational standards - no margins, single spaced, different sized and different coloured paper, no indents, word count, paragraphs or page numbers. Even if they were to disregard items like corrections, bad typing, and the handwritten scrawls all over the pages, there is not a great deal they can do with the manuscript other than return it to the author with a request that it be re-typed and presented correctly. "A lot of valuable time, money and energy can be saved by presenting a good clean manuscript", they concluded.

From The Editor's Desk workshops invite participants to submit work in advance so that an assessment can be given and the workshop tailored to suit specific needs. The over-riding factor, however, is that over 80% of those manuscripts would be instantly rejected by a majority of editors/publishers. It comes as a bit of a shock to eager, would-be writers to learn that their submissions are totally unacceptable by professional standards, but the point of the workshops is to try to get potential freelance writers *thinking* like professionals.

Even the *Quartos* postbag contains its fair share of poorly produced articles - and not all of these are submitted by non-subscribers. There are writers who have been with us for years who still insist on submitting barely legible text due to a worn out printer ribbon, or cramped, single spacing and no margins in order to save on paper. If their attitude is 'it doesn't matter, since it's only *Quartos*' then one suspects that it doesn't matter if it's only a small press publication, or a small competition. It matters! So rid yourself of the bad habits before it's too late.

The ground rules for presentation differ little between submitting a full length manuscript to an agent or publisher, a competition entry for judging, and a short story/article to an editor. The agency spokesman gave the following advice:

"NEVER submit a handwritten manuscript - although the occasional competition may state this is acceptable. When the final draft is being typed or wordprocessed, always ensure that a new *black* ribbon or ink cartridge is being used. Make sure that every page has an inch and a half wide margin and that every page is numbered. (Agent David Bolt's book tells the story of how his cat upset the entire manuscript of an unnumbered, full-length novel!).

Typing should always be double-spaced, ie. a FULL line of space between lines of copy, on standard A4 white paper. With full length works, a new chapter should begin halfway down on a new page, and the pages of each chapter clipped together. Never staple full length manuscript pages. Many editors or competition organis-ers do not object to stapling but your safest bet is to use a paper clip. And NEVER, NEVER use a dressmaker's pin which could result in blood-stained paper!

The cover or title page gives the title of the work, an approxi-mate word count and your name, address and telephone number, together with the rights you are offering, ie. FBSR - First British Serial Rights. If you must mark corrections, keep them to a minimum, otherwise your submission will start to look messy and no agent will submit a tatty, dog-eared manuscript to a publisher on your behalf - even if the content of the work has merit . Today's publishing world is about packaging, presentation and professionalism."

Another useful little 'insider' snippet comes from Joan Clayton in *Journalism For Beginners*. She informs us that only amateurs justify both left and right margins, ie. where all the words are aligned. "Editors hate it ... It may look smart at first glance, but it creates unnatural and confusing spaces between and within words ... Don't do it."

The Professional Viewpoint:

There's also a great deal of information to be learnt about the agents and publishers themselves before sending off that statutory synopsis and first two sample chapters with a covering letter. In an article published in an earlier issue of *Quartos*, two literary agents and a publisher gave their 'Top Ten Hit-List' for writers' gaffs - see how many you've made so far in submitting manuscripts for consideration.

The first on the list of all three were unsolicited novels with no return postage and no suitable package for its return. Needless to say, there were thumbs down for submissions full of inaccuracies in grammar, spelling, foreign quotations and facts, etc. This appears to be the most common problem and the most heavily criticised.

One of our agents has the distinct impression that a lot of 'authors' cannot be bothered to read their own work through, never mind edit it! "Don't they realise it is in their own interests to do so?" he stressed.

Writers who provide inadequate information about their work are also unpopular. All prefer to receive an author's c.v. including age, other work in hand and details of which other agents/ publishers have declined the book and not, as often happens, a covering letter simply stating "I have written a novel" and that is all. Unreadable pages full of alternations, tippex and coffee stains doesn't create a good impression either - all require clearly typed, double spaced on one side of the paper only, with pages numbered and securely fastened.

Random sample chapters submitted without a synopsis, any form of description or word count try the patience, as does a synopsis received with a covering letter but with no name or identification on the synopsis. A sample extract from Chapter 38 and a brief outline of a plot will tell them nothing.

All are irritated by unsolicited manuscripts outside the guidelines that have been clearly stated in the writers' reference books, while the second agent indicated a dislike of self-indulgent books of interest to nobody except the author.

Telephone enquires are not well received, especially if the author insists on explaining the entire plot of the novel; neither is material that has obviously been sent to a number of agencies/ publishers simultaneously. Our publisher objected to writers who expect editorial criticism to work of no interest to the publishing house and those with "unrealistic expectations of publication, either financial or concerned with instant notoriety". Similarly, our agents have little patience with those who expect a decision after five days, or believe that their first novel is worth £100,000!

Publisher are not interested in writers who talk about books which are not yet written, or those who only have one book in them - a sentiment endorsed by both agents, who only accepts young(ish) writers who wish to make a career out of writing and are not out to write a 'one-off'. Having signed the contract, publishers find that the author/publisher relationship is often put under pressure when deadlines are missed, or the author thinks three or four re-writes are too much work. Although his sympathies are very much with the writer, his first commitment is to stay in business so he will readily suggest changes if these could increase the saleability or re-duce costs - and expect the author to co-operate.

It appears that at all levels of writing, from initial tutorial to finished, full-length manuscript, it is extremely difficult to convince writers that they need to pay more attention to their submissions.

Janie Jackson:

"Some of my students get peeved when I insist that work is submitted to me in the correct professional format - double line spacing on one side only of plain A4 paper. I've had complaints that they enrolled for the course to learn how to write, not to take typing lessons. That's not the point. I'm trying to get my students into the habit of thinking like professionals, taking a pride in what they write and how it's presented. Remember - you never get a second chance to make a first impression.

Another problem is the type of envelope used for the return of student's work. Until I became a tutor, I assumed that anybody - and everybody - would use the size of envelope most suited to the pages it contained. In the beginning I was surprised when students sent an ordinary correspondence envelope for the return of a 20-page assignment. Others sent a C4 size (or even larger) for the return of two pages.

But the people who really bug me are those who send torn, coffee-stained, previously used envelopes. I'm all in favour of saving trees and I appreciate the need for economy - but I wonder how those students would feel if they were on the receiving end? One student was genuinely surprised when I protested about a filthy crumpled envelope with a much-licked and ripped open flap. Next time she sent me something similar - but had neatly slit along the flap so that there was no means of sealing it."

In the course of organising four national writing competitions Margaret Finch had handled over 2500 manuscripts and as many requests for entry forms. Just when she thought she had seen it all, along came another little quirk to take her by surprise - like the postcard stating 's.a.e enclosed'. Or the 9x4" s.a.e folded into a thick wad secured with a paper clip, inside a large envelope with a note on an inch wide scrap of paper!

"When a competition was in progress I sometimes had to, pick up around thirty letters scattered over my porch floor. To save time, the obvious junk mail was discard immediately, so it was only by chance that one gaudy 'Let's fix your pix' envelope turned over in the bin to disclose a command to save trees addressed to me."

"Actually, I'm going off this tree-saving business," she continued, "when I think of the extra tonnage of non-biodegradable sellotape involved. It takes 43" to reinforce the edges of a second-hand A4 envelope and more to bind the folded surfaces together. The resulting impenetrable packs, often thick and shiny, poses the problem of whether to use a Stanley knife, red hot poker or hacksaw to get at the contents."

The list is endless and in case you think we are exaggerating, the foibles of competition entrants has provided Margaret Finch with enough material for *four* full-length articles for different writing magazines on the subject.

One reader did not advocate using recycled paper for manuscripts, "If you want to impress an editor, only the best will do." This brought a prompt response from another reader who did not agree with her fellow writer's sentiments about impressing editors.

"If your submission isn't good enough, it won't be accepted no matter how fancy or expensive your paper! Editors are only impressed with a good story or article, that is neatly and cleanly presented. Recycled paper is quite adequate providing it's not coloured ..."

Fancy plastic folders and tarty folios don't score any points either, and during a competition, the variety of styles and types of folder can be truly amazing. Several regular *Quartos* contributors enclose their articles in clear plastic folders, together with an A4 envelope for return, and from a personal point of view, it does help to keep the whole lot together, but for national competition organisers or editors, they are nothing but a nuisance and usually get discarded as soon as they arrive. The reason behind this extravagant gesture is that it is almost impossible to stack manuscripts that are encased in plastic folders; at the slightest nudge, they take off like exocet missiles. The first prize for extravagance, however, should go to the entrant who sent a short story encased in a black shiny plastic holder with the title, etc carefully emblazoned in gold Lettraset!

Once you have prepared your manuscript and the final draft is ready for submission, put it away for a week, or even a month! It is quite amazing how you can suddenly think of a new twist to a sentence, or recall a glaring error once the wretched thing is nestling at the bottom of the post-box. After a while, bring it out of the drawer again and re-read it; make your alterations and if you haven't already thought about it, add that eye-catching title.

Author of many published articles, Shirley Read stressed the importance of using the right title. "In choosing your title, you need to consider the type of magazine to which you are submitting the article. What might be acceptable to the lighter, frothier publication could be frowned upon if suggested to a more serious magazine, even if the subject matter and/or style in which the piece was written happened to suit both." Study the titles used by your chosen magazine as a guide to whether the editor appreciates punning, parodies, quotes, etc.

John Copley added "A minor art in its own right, titling ... One effective and often used ploy is to take some well-known and cliched phrase and twist it slightly. Twist it more than slightly, if necessary to make it mean the exact opposite to the original while, of course, still retaining enough of the original for it to be instantly recognised."

Writers' magazines are the places to find these handy hints on how to develop a more professional approach to your writing, although how-to books might mention them in passing. For example, a beginner would never think of sending half a dozen article suggestions to an editor, but according to journalist and editor, Christine Hall, this is exactly the approach you *should* adopt if you don't want to give the impression of being an amateur.

Christine Hall:

"When writing to offer feature articles that might be of interest, use the opportunity to submit multiple suggestions. They show the freelance has studied the publication, is interested in the subject, qualified to write about it and could become a regular contributor ... If the first ideas list contains nothing suitable but the freelance shows promise, an editor will always explain and ask for more ideas.

One word of warning if you intend approaching an editor with an outline for an article prior to submission, don't identify yourself as an amateur by proposing a length that is inadequate to cover the subject. Prepare a rough outline estimating how many words are needed to cover each point and give yourself a wide margin on either side. The editor's response will inform you how much space he's willing to allocate."

When submitting full-length work to a publisher or agent NEVER send the complete manuscript in the first instance - if you do it will only land up on the slush pile and take months to return. *The Writer's Handbook* and *The Writers' & Artists' Year Book* outline the requirements of publishers, who mostly require two sample chapters and a detailed synopsis, together with a curriculum vitae and return postage.

Take as much trouble preparing the synopsis as you did with the manuscript because this will be the only indication a publisher has of your capabilities as a potential author. In fact, it will be necessary for you to create the story in miniature, although the synopsis should do more than merely summarise the plot or subject. It is the synopsis that whets the publisher's appetite for more and the one that is poorly thought out or boring, is asking for a rejection slip.

Similarly your c.v. should give the publisher all he needs to know about your *writing career* to date. This does not include the school essay on the ancestry of your grandmother's parrot; list your successes clearly and concisely, including any other full-length works you have in hand. As we have already seen, publishers do not like to accept 'one-off' authors who may not be able to produce another book, so let them know you are already working on another manuscript and give brief details, even if it's only in the ideas/planning stage. Keep your covering letter short and polite, and don't clutter it up with unnecessary information.

When submitting your manuscripts to a publisher/agent for the first time make sure you are including everything he needs - so refer to this check-list before sealing the envelope:

* A brief covering letter
* Chapters one and two
* The synopsis
* Your curriculum vitae (c.v.)
* A stamped addressed envelope
* A stamped addressed postcard for acknowledgement

A stamped addressed envelope is a must for all submissions but even this doesn't guarantee that the recipient will respond to your enquiry, and may even claim at a later stage that the manuscript was never received. If you accept that a book proposal of any size can remain 'under consideration' for quite a long time, you nevertheless would still like to know that it has been received safely.

Either enclose a stamped addressed *postcard* for the recipient to signed and return, or send the manuscript by Recorded Delivery Service via the Post Office. The sender fills in a certificate of posting which is handed over with a completed 'Advice of Delivery' card at the Post Office for franking. The sender retains the franked certificate (stick it on the back of the copy letter, or on the relevant date in that large desk diary). As proof of posting you will receive the relevant portion of the 'Advice of Delivery' card by 1st class mail as soon as it has been delivered and signed for. If there is any later argument as to whether your package or letter was delivered, you have the actual proof in your possession.

Think in terms of your presentation being an extension of yourself. Show that you are clean and tidy in your work, prompt with your delivery, ready to oblige, courteous and most importantly of all, prepared to behave in a professional manner. Writers never believe the amount of rubbish that publishers and editors receive. There must be hundreds of tons of paper lying around editorial offices that no one can bring themselves to look at, because of the disgusting state of the manuscripts. Remember that the cavalier treatment frequently complained about *by writers* is not necessarily the whole of the story.

Copyright:

Participants at workshops frequently express their concern over who owns the copyright on their work and often ask what they can do to safeguard their ideas from being stolen. Of course, there are horror stories of similar pieces being discovered in a magazine some time after the original writer submitted his/her manuscript to a competition or editor. It does happen - but rarely. Nevertheless it is important to understand what is covered by copyright.

Firstly, your work is safeguarded by the Copyright Act from the moment you type 'The End' and date the piece. You can mail yourself a copy by Registered Post and keep the sealed envelope tucked away somewhere safe in case you need to prove any dispute that may arise. There are even agencies offering to register your work under the Copyright Act but think very carefully before you begin to spend money to protect yourself from potential literary thieves. If your story or article *has* been stolen the best you're going to get is an apology from the editor. They may not use the other freelance again but unless you've got money to burn, litigation is going to be expensive, if all that is at stake is a 2500 word short story.

Secondly, *ideas* are not protected by copyright so be extremely careful with whom you discuss the details of your next project - as Joan Clayton points out, if they get the book written before yours is completed, then the copyright belongs to them! The Society of Authors produce a series of low cost pamphlets on copyright and other legal aspects of writing, so send a s.a.e and ask for details of the publications available.

Rejection Slips

Every writer receives his or her fair share of rejections slips, and next to writers' block is also the favourite subject of beginner article writers. There can, however, be a wealth of hidden information in the TYPE of rejection slips that accompany your returned manuscript(s). Don't just disregard them, think about the editor's comments and glean whatever information you can before filing, or throwing them away.

If an editor states that this particular piece isn't right for them, but they would be interested to consider other submissions - go back to your research copies and work at getting it right for next time. If a publisher makes enthusiastic comments about your novel whilst saying that the subject/genre is unsuitable for their list, go back to *The Writer's Handbook* and find one who it will suit. 'Editor-speak' can be obtuse in the extreme but unless an editor feels compelled to make some observation, s/he won't bother out of politeness.

As John Copley explained "The standard, ready-printed ones aren't much use. All they tell you is that you've blown out yet again, but the rarer ones, when some busy editor is decent enough to add a few words of helpful comment are like gold. It can be a suggestion for a change to the piece, or even a pointer towards another potential market. "Not quite right for us, try *'Plonk'* magazine." Don't be too upset if it duly comes whizzing back from *'Plonk'* too, together with a helpful note that the first magazine you tried might take it. It's nice of them to take the trouble, and if you can't take the odd joke, you shouldn't have joined the scribbling racket."

The most flattering rejection I have personally received came from a London agent, who responded to my own synopsis and sample chapters with: "... I must therefore recommend you to try elsewhere, but I wish you luck. Your presentation incidentally is excellent; just what an agent wants to know ..." Obviously a man who understands that a few well-chosen words can work wonders for jaded spirits - and who was willing to write an encouraging personal letter in response.

When Ann Cook received a letter from an interested publisher with a request for her home telephone number she was heavily pregnant, so the letter was filed away. Many months later, when tidying out her writing drawer, she came across the letter and read it properly. Because the publisher had not said "Yes" but ... "there is a great deal I should like to see done ...", Ann had taken it as a rejection. If you are lucky enough to get a long letter back with your manuscript, instead of a terse rejection slip then READ IT and if it says 'phone - DO!

Before becoming too disheartened, consider the fact that the majority of the now famous have, in their time, also received their fair share of disappointments. Barbara Erskine's *Lady of Hay*, which eventually sold 125,000 copies in the UK alone, was finally accepted on its 44th submission. Rejection slips are an important part of your market research, so don't just take them at their face value - but please don't turn them into another article for your favourite writing magazine!

Simultaneous Submissions:

We also receive numerous queries from writers asking about submitting work to more than one agent/publisher at a time and asking why this practice is frowned upon. The question of the simultaneous submission is a double edged sword and one not easily put in perspective.

On one hand we have a business situation where a supplier (you, the writer) is being told you can only sell to one customer (editor/ publisher) at a time; on the other, you are the supplier who needs a quick response on order to offer your wares to another customer with a minimum of delay. In either case the turn-around period can be anything from 6 weeks to 6 months - not a viable business proposal in anyone's book. If you play by the rules, it means that your novel or full-length non-fiction is only going to be seen by (at worst) two or (at best) eight potential buyers in the course of a year.

Writing is also part of the publishing *business*, so send off as many synopses + two sample chapters as outlets/finances allow and accept right from the start that it's going to take longer to sell it than write it ... and there aren't any short cuts. Keep a strict diary of submissions, returns, rejects, comments, etc., and if you haven't had a response within 4-6 weeks (depending on the type of manuscript), submit elsewhere.

Once a publisher has requested to see the rest of the book, however, it is unprofessional to send off a full-length copy elsewhere, even if it's been requested. Wait six weeks and if you haven't heard from the first publisher, send it off to the second together with a covering letter stating which other publisher is showing an interest. Hedge your bets and work on a first come, first served basis but do allow a realistic period of time before re-submitting. Follow-up letters asking if they are interested in taking your book are usually a waste of valuable writing time, so get busy on your next project

Do bear in mind that if you then decide to approach an agent, you will have to list *every* publisher already contacted. And having covered every relevant one in *The Writers' Handbook* and *The Writers' & Artists' Yearbook* yourself, face the fact that your newly acquired agent is going to have a difficult, if not impossible task of selling your manuscript. Even agents can't work miracles.

It is inadvisable to submit material to more than one agent at a time because agents aren't in the position to *accept* manuscripts for publication. They need time to cast their nets around the publishing houses to see if anyone is interested in taking up your novel or non-fiction. On finding an agent, don't continue to submit to publishers because you'll only land up making yourself and your agent appear foolish in the eyes of the publishing houses. You should have some sort of response with 4-6 weeks and if you haven't, you *can* write again asking politely for information.

Articles and short stories should, of course, be tailored to suit each individual editor but having submitted a manuscript for consideration, allow four weeks before re-writing and submitting elsewhere. It could be embarrassing all round if an identical article or short story appears in two different magazines, and it won't help your reputation as a responsible writer. It is permissible, however, to submit two articles on the same topic, but *slanted from a different angle* to two different magazines.

Agents:

One of the most common questions asked by writers is: "How do I go about finding myself an agent?" Why have new writers become brainwashed into needing the services of an agent even before the ink on the notes of their first full-length book has had time to dry?

... Because for years publishers and agents have perpetuated the myth that in order to be published you need to submit your work through a literary agent. The real advantages in this triangle are firmly loaded on the side of the publisher who hopes that by stating "Manuscripts should only be submitted via an agent", his slush pile will be reduced. This is understandable in view of a recent newspaper article which revealed that a well-known publishing house received about 15,000 unsolicited manuscripts, proposals and synopses a year, and that the average rate of acceptance is $0.05\% = 1$ in 2000 for that particular imprint.

Publishers know that manuscripts pre-read by a professional will not be a complete waste of their time, but it is important to realise that no publisher is going to turn down a potential hit because it hasn't come via an agency. In *Write A Successful Novel* (co-authored with Moe Sherrard-Smith), prolific novelist Frederick Smith devotes some eleven pages of guidance on the subject for would-be authors and recommends that for a first novel, the writer should approach a publisher direct - and forget about a third party representing your interests.

In an article published in *Quartos*, Ann Cook wrote that she had reached the conclusion that *she* would rather search for dragons, than try to find herself an agent. The first one she approached stated that she welcomed newcomers, so she sat down and carefully typed up a c.v., putting down every choice morsel she could dredge up as bait. Within a week she received a reply - the agency felt Ann was on her way to the top but could only deal with her adult novels.

"Fine, but I hadn't written any! They did feel that my teenage fantasy might just qualify BUT another agency who dealt with short stories, children's books, etc ., might suit me better since I wrote so widely. They very kindly recommended a couple."

Another to whom Ann had written nibbled at the bait. "Send whatever is representative of your work, she said. "Two weeks later she wasn't 'enthusiastic enough' about my work to represent me and wished me luck.   In the same post as the refusal came a commission which has now been accepted along with the short story I sent out with it on spec. So if agents don't like my work, somebody seems to!"

By the next issue, we'd managed to catch a literary spokeswoman who was willing to reveal the secrets behind getting yourself an agent (or rather, how NOT to ...). "Approach is all," she announced. "The problem stems, initially from a lack of editorial discretion ... on the writer's part rather than the publishers.   Publishers are inundated with manuscripts and can spot an amateur long before they've jemmied open the padded envelope. A professional can remove many of the obstacles and smooth the way but you'll need to convince them of your merit and literary prowess.   We're looking for marketable material and for writers with a strong sense of commitment to their craft; we're not looking for one-offs, or autobiographies, unless of course, you happen to be famous or, better still, infamous!"

Let The Writer Beware!

Having wasted two years at the mercy of a London agent, I would endorse Frederick Smith's sentiments and now tend to view the majority of them (with notable exceptions) in the same light that I would double-glazing salesmen! Following acceptance by the agency in January 1989, I forwarded the complete manuscript and was even invited to the office for lengthy discussions about my plans for future books. By March 1991, I had completed my second book and forwarded the outline which was immediately accepted with some enthusiasm, although there were a few suggestions for a partial re-write - it was also confirmed that the first manuscript was being considered by its fourth publisher.

By September 1991 the re-write of the second book was completed and posted. A telephone call and a highly complimentary letter followed almost by return of post but that's the last I ever heard of either manuscripts or agent. Despite letters, fax and telephone calls neither manuscript had been returned; but that wasn't the *real* problem ...

Because both books had been submitted to several different publishers, I couldn't re-submit them elsewhere because the agent also ignored my requests to be informed of the publishers already contacted; and since any potential outlet would almost certainly ask who else had seen the manuscript, I found myself in the possession of 350 useless pages of novel and 250 pages of unsaleable non-fiction. This is because many publishers are chary about considering something which has been turned down by the opposition unless they know who's seen it.

Mine was not an isolated instance since several *Quartos* readers, having completed full-length manuscripts have suffered similar cavalier treatment from literary agencies - all of them still appearing year after year in the writers' reference books.

Following the publication of the above extract in *Quartos*, the missing manuscripts were finally returned by the agency. No word of explanation, no apology, no indication as to why the long silence - four years in all! So my advice would still be: "Don't waste time touting for an agent if you're working on your first book. If you're a serious writer, get down to the business in hand; write and study your marketplace. Learn how to prepare a manuscript for submission, take your time in getting it right - and go to the publisher direct. This, of course, is my own *personal* opinion and the article prompted Graham Stevenson to give his opposing views on dealing through an agent:

Graham Stevenson:

"There is nothing wrong with marketing yourself, of course. But there is nothing wrong with letting the *right* agency do it for you either. It depends on your needs. After putting my first book proposal together I submitted it to sixteen publishers with the same result: rejection. Fortunately, the seventeenth recommended an agent and within six weeks, my newly acquired representative had negotiated a contract. He sold my second book idea in an even shorter period. The fact that my proposals had been presented by an agent gave them sufficient edge to be accepted.

Having a professional representative leaves you free to get on with other things. A small percentage of a writer's time is taken up with the writing process itself - selling eats up a good proportion too. If you appoint an agent you have more time to write. They also know how to sell subsidiary rights, including overseas versions. Mine recently sold the Indonesian rights in my latest book. Would you begin to know how to do that on your own?

An agent has to give you an edge. A good one that is ... Ideally, you will be introduced by recommendation but if you're not that fortunate, you'll have to go it alone. Unfortunately the writers' handbooks don't have a grading system but those belonging to the Association of Author's Agents will have to abide by its code of practice. As we've said, whether or not you need an agent depends upon your point of view. The bottom line is if you want to use one, use one. If you don't, don't."

Ironically, two days after the missing manuscripts turned up, *The Author* published a detailed report on UK agents and the one who had caused me so much hassle was included high on The

Society of Author's list of highly commended agents. (All those complained about by our readers also belong to the A.A.A.) Of the 5,600 members of the Society, apparently half do not use the services of a literary agency and of the 494 responding to the questionnaire, the majority were satisfied with the service.

Despite the problems caused by falling prey to an inefficient agency, I would certainly *prefer* to hand the whole marketing process over to a reliable one, but having wasted time on re-writing two complete manuscripts, I'm reluctant to lose control over knowing who is reading them (if anyone at all) and not being informed of any positive/negative feedback. Both manuscripts were submitted at an agent's invitation - neither were unsolicited.

In the meantime, I'm carrying on with my current books; should an agent eventually undertake the marketing of my work, he will have to come up with some pretty impressive recommendations, and not just a listing in the writers' guides. To be fair to the profession, however, I asked both Moe Sherrard-Smith and Merric Davidson to give their views and advice on approaching them:

Moe Sherrard-Smith:

"Take time to study the available writers' guides and make a short list of those who deal in fiction. If clients' names are listed against an agency's name, then consider whether your kind of literature fits that general type of list. If you're writing funny and salacious satire in modern jargon and tone, then those handling highly polished and sedate literary fiction is unlikely to want to take you on.

If you're friendly with published writers ask them, discreetly, about who acts for them. Word of mouth can be a good form of recommendation and an easy route to a name. Remember, not all agents advertise in the guides and finding the ones who don't is a harder task. A 'phone call is the best initial approach as it will save unnecessary time and postage if the books are full, or your work is not in his field of operation/expertise.

Be polite, be prepared. Jot down the points you wish to raise: state the book's genre and length; have one or two paragraphs of sharp and succinct synopsis ready so you can explain that the book's about. List your previous writing history, if any. Ask if they will read some, or all, of your script. Ask if (as many agencies are doing now) he charges a reading fee. If so, what it is. Are you prepared to pay it? £10 or £15 may not be unrealistic, but £40 or £50 is serious money, when the end result may still be rejection.

Listen carefully whilst you're talking. The author-agent relationship needs to be mutual if it is to work. If you can't empathise with the voice and manner of the person on the other end on the 'phone, it will, in all likelihood, be doomed to failure.

Agents, like publishers, are always too busy, and many agencies do close their lists from time to time. If you are turned away because their books are full, don't misconstrue it as rejection of your script, or you as a writer. There are only 24 hours in a day and it takes time and commitment to service an author's work whole-heartedly and honestly. Some agents simply have no more time available.

Don't be disheartened, keep at it. Move down your list of possibilities and try the next name. Ironically, if you've gone directly to a publisher with your script, and elicited some interest in it, even perhaps a tentative offer or invitation to 'talk about it' - that's the time to tell it to an agent who may well be prepared to take on a newcomer."

Merric Davidson:

"What I like is a professional, straight forward, typed cover letter which tells me all I need to know. Background is important. Briefly, the letter should state what the book is about (plus a *slightly* longer synopsis), why the book was written plus a glimpse at the perceived market, any previous successes in print - doesn't matter what, and a paragraph on the writer rather than a huge c.v. That's the best advice. Keep it simple but fact-filled.

Oh, and make sure in advance that you're sending the right material to the right agent. There are certain categories of fiction that I don't handle and a lot more in the case of non-fiction."

Equally as important as understanding the correct method of approaching an agent as a prospective client, is knowing exactly what drives them round the bend ...

Moe Sherrard -Smith:

"Usually would-be authors who are not experienced enough, or have never really written anything. That is, they have a vague idea they would like to write a novel (mainly in the mistaken belief that there are millions to be made!), but aren't even sure whether they can, or what genre they want to tackle; and - "Could I just have a chat with you so you can point me in the right direction." That sort of chat is invariably over-long and totally unproductive. Or the eager beaver who has "written a masterpiece and I want you to be the first to look at it so you can correct the English and odd things before you get it published." I may suggest overall changes to a script with a view to improving its *commercial quality* or marketability and hint at corrections to the language but I'm not a copy-editor, nor a teacher of English. Coupled with these, of course, go the sloppily presented, dog-eared, ill-typed scripts that really don't impress me and certainly won't impress a publisher. I don't have the time (or the inclination) to get out a magnifying glass and high powered torch to read a script which has only had the faintest of contact with a printing ribbon. And unless you truly *have* written that rare thing, the masterpiece, sloppy presentation is invariably indicative of the state of the writing. Similarly, an endless stream of 'phone calls to check on the progress of a script, is irritating in the extreme - and only delays me further."

Merric Davidson:

"What sort of approach drives me round the bend? Probably the 'usual' - any letter which begins, 'This is your lucky day ...'. And then there's the comic cuts letter which is equally off-putting. You just know at a glance that could *never* work with anyone who thinks you've got the time for a good laugh, particularly on a bad Monday. Really, it pays to let your writing do the talking. That's the only thing that counts after all."

Political Correctness:

As if we didn't have enough to worry about. Having experimented with a different genre to my usual supernatural chillers, I've recently completed a rather raunchy little 80,000 word novel which I sent to an agency inviting, and specialising in, 'women's writing'. The response was that, although the plot was good she 'couldn't love the characters enough' due to the lack of political correctness in the opinions expressed in the dialogue of the four principle women players.

Editors and publishers are now constantly on the look-out for infringements of political correctness and will reject or request a re-write if they feel that the text does not conform with the trend for PC pruning. As *The Daily Telegraph* recently reported: "Once upon a time novelists could write what they liked but, in the age of political correctness, established writers and first-timers like Jane Gordon have to be aware of offending readers."

Apparently Ms Gordon has been left wondering if she is suited to the writing of contemporary fiction having been accused by her copy editor of being 'lookist, fatist, elitist and 'insulting to women'. Now it is considered politically incorrect to call women 'girls' or 'ladies' although novelist Alice Thomas Ellis persists because she considers it rude to be referred to as a woman. The list is endless but established authors such as Maeve Haran, Dick Francis, Celia Brayfield, Jilly Cooper and Kingley Amis have all felt the cutting effects of the copy editor's politically correct blue pencil.

Children's books face the closest scrutiny of all and those looking for a career in this particular genre should pay very close attention to what is available on the library shelves. Many old favourites have already been cannibalised to make them suitable for today's children so pay particular attention to your market research if you want to get it right.

The majority of workshop participants (mostly ladies of all ages) think it is utterly ridiculous that women writers can be accused of sexism *towards other women*, or that *The Famous Five* have been surgically altered for the benefit of 1990s children, but for the moment this is the way of the publishing world and publishers are bowing to the demands of political correctness.   If you don't take a national newspaper that has a weekly Books & Arts section (weekend editions of the *Telegraph* or *Times*, for example), ask friends to pass on their copies because this will keep you up-to-date with current publishing news and the social trends which are affecting the acceptable tone of contemporary mainstream fiction.

Recommended Reading:

Sadly *An Author's Handbook* by David Bolt has been dropped from Piatkus's book list; personally speaking I think it is still one of the most valuable books for would-be authors.   Written after thirty years as a bookseller, publisher's reader, author and literary agent, David Bolt published a book that tells you all you need to know about preparing and presenting manuscripts, and how best to approach agents and publishers.   It should still be available through a reliable booksearch.

How To Be A Freelance Journalist by Christine Hall. Written from the editor's viewpoint, this book is an invaluable source of insider knowledge for beginners and professionals with the author revealing the best-selling feature subjects, and what editors really want. This much needed book contains everything you've always wanted to know: from writing irresistible query letters to how to cope with difficult interviewees, from infallible formulas for feature writing to how to illustrate your articles. Commissioning editors of magazines such as *Chat, Good Housekeeping* and *Woman* explain what they are looking for. ISBN 185703 147 4. (How To Books Limited - Plymouth)

Chapter 5   Writing Fiction

In his novel *Stop Press*, Michael Innes gave two of his characters the following dialogue:

"Do you know how a best-seller comes into being?"

"Certainly not."

"Nor does anyone else. Do you know why people don't buy books?"

"Well, approximately - yes."

"... But when they do buy a book do you know why they do it?"

"I have no idea at all."

"Exactly. And neither has anyone else ..."

Whilst written pre-war, the sentiments expressed are probably still true - *no-one does know* what it takes to write a best seller, despite the numerous how-to books on the subject. On an even more depressing note, the market-place for fiction is so over-subscribed that it is almost impossible to advise new writers where to submit material with a reasonable chance of publication.

Each of us write in a particular *genre* - the category/subject area into which our story fits - and it is essential to identify this category as early as possible, since it gives a clearly defined picture of where we will ultimately try to sell our short stories and novels. For example, if we want to write science fiction or horror, we must familiarise ourselves with *everything* that has been published in that field from the early days of the genre right up to the present day. Why? Because we need to know and recognise these antecedents if we are going to attempt something new and exciting to offer to a publisher or editor.

In another rather innocuous thriller published in 1939, one of the characters reflects ... "The whole subject of the uncanny is certainly fascinating. And uncommonly good material for imaginative writing. When you come to think of it all the world's great stories have an element of the supernatural. Its abandonment means the sacrifice of a great many good story-telling effects." Nevertheless, the 'chiller' writer who *hasn't* studied Machen, Stoker, Shelley and Poe will lack a certain insight or 'feel' for his subject.

Under the same banner, we find the ever popular ghost story, which appears in all types of publications from the *Bella* minimystery to whole anthologies, though the ghost story has never been treated with the scorn often reserved for the rest of the horror genre. Perhaps the secret of the true supernatural chiller/ghost story is compulsion. The twilight world of the supernatural has intrigued mankind for thousands of years, with the reader being irresistibly drawn towards the instrument of his own terror; there must always be the forces of empathy and repellent fascination. Even so, there's a lot of original thought needed to bring the ghost story up-to-date in the late 1990s - a rehash of traditional themes is not enough for today's editor who is looking for originality in the telling.

Similarly at the other end of the scale, if you think you want to write romance, Janie Jackson still advises beginners to define the term in their own minds before tackling a full-length novel. "Genre novels apart, romantic fiction must surely also include 'confessions'; some of the short stories and serials in women's magazines; and the cheap paperbacks (i.e *My Weekly Library*, etc.). Perhaps the newcomer to this field of writing would be well advised to cut her teeth on this type of work. It can be rewarding, financially and otherwise." In other words, familiarise yourself with your chosen genre before bombarding editors and publishers with full-length manuscripts.

Whereas the market for adventure, westerns, horror and science fiction can be extremely limiting, the wide outlet for romantic/ domestic/historical short stories and serials can be found in the national women's magazines, although more and more are no longer accepting freelance contributions. If your writing interests fall within this category, send for the complete set of guidelines for the D. C. Thomson stable from The Central Fiction Department at Albert Square, Dundee DD1 9QL.

Janie Jackson:
"If romance is your forte, why not consider submitting your novel in serial form to one of the weekly magazines which usually include a serial as part of its regular fiction slot. Varying from publication to publication, the opening instalment is usually between 5-7000 words and must end with a 'cliff-hanger' to encourage the reader to purchase the next week's issue.

The following instalments are generally around 5000 but the overall length depends on the individual editor, so plenty of opportunity for market research here. Be warned however, just because the manuscript appears in serial form in a weekly magazine does not mean that the editor will accept inferior writing. Some very important writers have appeared in the serialised form over the years."

For full-length fiction in the same genre, Mills & Boon have a most voracious appetite and the commissioning editors are willing to work with new writers if you have potential; they also produce excellent guidelines which help you to understand exactly what they are looking for in new writers. In every case you must make a practice of reading the fiction *currently* being published by these outlets by checking the publishing date on the inside - writing for them is not as easy as it looks!

'Confession' magazines are also considered good paying outlets for freelance writers and are not necessarily confined solely to female writers. Several male *Quartos* readers have had stories accepted by women's confession publications.

Two fiction markets that are not so well known are the photo-stories and picture story range of which D. C. Thomson (and others) publish dozens of titles. Both the photo and picture story is a complete story in itself, not just an incident or summary. It has to have a story shape with an intriguing start, a development of plot and atmosphere, and a rounding-up finish. Script writing for photo and picture stories has much in common with the writing of scenarios for films or television and D. C. Thomson are always interested in new writers. Both offer the opportunity to write for markets that may not have occurred to you before (romance and children); those which no longer appear to be popular with mainstream publishers (war, adventure and sport); or difficult to break into (science fiction).

The full-length adventure story may, in some quarters, be considered passe but if you have a talent for story-telling in this genre and find your markets limited, why not send for 'Scriptwriting for D. C. Thomson' or 'Some Hints on Writing Photo-Stories' which give examples on how to write and present a script. The company publishes a range of picture story papers for both boys and girls in the 7-12 age group; *Star Love Story Library*; *Commando Libraries* and *Star Blazer Libraries* (science fiction), while photo stories are aimed at readers in their teens.

Unfortunately, those writing short stories in other genres are largely confined to the small independent presses (see Chapter 9) and Competitions (see Chapter 8), where off-beat, experimental or non-genre fiction is more sympathetically viewed. In addition, there are several outlets amongst the small presses for horror and science fiction, ranging from first class to the mediocre. Again, most of these outlets are usually tracked down through your chosen writers' magazine though very few offer any form of payment other than complimentary copies.

From time to time good fiction magazines appear but since there are more people wanting to write for them than there are subscribers, the life span of some can be extremely short. One magazine offering an outlet for highly readable contemporary fiction is the Arts Council funded *Metropolitan*, which calls itself 'the new magazine of urban short stories'. Other established publications such as *Staple* or the *Tees Valley WRITER* offer a prestigious showcase for new writers' fiction. Geoff Carroll's

Writers' Guide also produces a booklet which is constantly updated and gives details of over 100 short story outlets for both the national, mainstream and small press magazines.

To get a feel for what is currently finding favour amongst competition judges and editors, try a year's subscription to *Acclaim Magazine* and the winners anthology, published each year by the **New Writers' Club** after the results of the Ian St. James Awards have been announced. While the fiction used by *Acclaim* is taken from the runners-up in the competition, the diverse interests and backgrounds of the readers and judges, ensure that those shortlisted run the whole gamut of fictional appreciation - fantasy, social comment, romance, murder, science fiction, horror, crime, etc. *Acclaim* provides new fiction writers with fine examples of contemporary writing without the confines of genre or editorial preference.

Essential ingredients: Theme & Plot

The Polti theory maintains that there are only 36 dramatic situations on which the writer of fiction can draw. By using single situations or several combinations, the basic theme of every story (long or short) ever told, written or devised can be summed up in the following list:

1. Supplication
2. Deliverance
3. Crime pursued by vengeance
4. Vengeance taken for kindred upon kindred
5. Pursuit
6. Disaster
7. Falling prey to cruelty or misfortune
8. Revolt
9. Daring enterprise
10. Abduction
11. The enigma
12. Obtaining
13. Enmity of kinsmen

98

14. Rivalry of kinsmen
15. Murderous adultery
16. Madness
17. Fatal imprudence
18. Involuntary crimes of love
19. Slaying of a kinsman unrecognised
20. Self sacrifice for an ideal
21. Self sacrifice for kindred
22. All sacrificed for passion
23. Necessity of sacrificing loved ones.
24. Rivalry of superior and inferior
25. Adultery
26. Crimes of love
27. Discovery of the dishonour of a loved one
28. Obstacles to love
29. An enemy loved
30. Ambition
31. Conflict with God
32. Mistaken jealousy
33. Erroneous judgement
34. Remorse
35. Recovery of a lost one
36. Loss of a loved one.

For editor/reader appeal, all fiction - novel or short story - needs a credible plot, a plausible theme, an original location and principal characters who, whilst being sharp, intelligent and successful, need to possess a few faults and foibles to give them added dimension.

Exotic or original locations can give a story an extra boost. Colin Dexter, the creator of Inspector Morse introduced us to the esoteric world of Academe by casting his plots amongst the traditions and dreamy spires of Oxford University life, while Simon Raven did the same for Cambridge. Dick Francis came up with his own original formula set amongst the racing fraternity where wealth frequently rubs shoulders with the lower echelons of society. Jilly

Cooper opened up the world of show jumping and polo, before turning her attentions on an international orchestra. Ellis Peters goes back to medieval Britain.

Lewis Hosegood:
"Every story should contain both theme and plot. Yet many people seem to confuse the two when asked to outline them. They are certainly not the same.

The THEME is concerned with its general attitude, its tone, its subject matter - its message if you like. Often this can be summed up in a single abstract noun - jealousy, revenge, wish-fulfilment, escape, ambition, remorse and so on. Or perhaps it could be summarised in a saying: 'Rags to Riches ... Beauty is but skin deep ...' The latter could be enlarged to: 'Even an unprepossessing girl with spirit can win through to happiness'. This might be the theme of *Jane Eyre, Rebecca, Cinderella* and indeed many romantic novels.

Sometimes the THEME can well be summed up in the title. *War & Peace, Gone With The Wind, Pride & Prejudice, Hard Times, The End Of The Affair, The Flight From The Enchanter.* The Victorians loved their explanatory titles (Hardy gave *Tess* the sub-title 'The Story of a Wronged Woman' which caused outrage) but today we tend to favour those which are more oblique.

The PLOT is concerned with precisely how the THEME is put into effect. A summary of the PLOT should take us through it step by step. How was the woman wronged? How did war and peace come to dictate the destiny of two families? How were they hard times? How was the arrogant pride of the South suddenly gone with the wind?

Some writers like to PLOT their work meticulously in advance; others prefer the freedom of letting it grow organically, as it were. But one should never lose sight of the THEME. A useful compromise is to map out in advance a series of 'stepping stones' - essential events or turning points in the story. Keep your eye firmly on these (and the conclusion) and you can navigate the rest.

Returning to our idea of THEME (escape or deliverance for example), we can also think of it as the core, or kernel, of a fruit, surrounded by edible flesh - the PLOT development. We could now break it down further by asking ourselves: What is the protagonist escaping from? Danger? Boredom? Reality? Responsibility? Guilt? Retribution? Begin to fill this out in your mind and the fruit ripens. Detail will suggest itself.

But let's never forget that all stories start with **Character**. Think of a character, visualise him/her intimately. (Ruth Rendell says she often begins with an arresting face, a portrait seen in a gallery, or someone in a crowd). Put that person in a **Setting** (also well visualised), introduce **Conflict** (usually another character or frustration) and you're off. Remember that **Character** should never be dependent on PLOT but vice versa. Work on the principle of "What might happen if ... ?" Then add a few twists and difficulties to overcome on the way. It rarely fails."

Characterisation:

Creating a whole cast of characters for your first book usually presents little difficulty. It is acknowledged that most first novels are autobiographical in that main characters reflect the thoughts and reactions of their author. The supporting cast are also readily assembled, drawn from a lifetime's garnering of friends, family, colleagues and chance acquaintances. They are all there, filed away in your subconscious, waiting for you to turn them into fictional players in your first drama or romance.

But what of subsequent novels? Or the casting for short stories? How is it possible to create a fresh set of players? How many times have you suffered disappointment when a favourite author's third or fourth book turns out to be a thinly disguised re-hash of previous characters, dished up with a different sauce? Learn from your own criticism of other authors, strip those used and familiar personnel out of your mental files, and create a set of new ones.

So - where can you find can you find a completely new cast to replace the ones who took a life-time to assemble? One secret is *casting*. Unless characters appear, unbidden and ready-formed from the deep recesses of the mind, try to imagine which actors you would select to play the parts if the story were transposed into a film or

101

television script. You will already have a rough idea of what your characters should be like, so try to find an actor who has played a similar part, or who would be likely to fit the role you're trying to create.

If you feel this idea is far fetched, admit how many times you've been exasperated by a casting director's decision to cast a particular actor in a part - particularly if it happens to be an adaptation of a favourite novel. All you are doing is reversing the process. It is essential, however, that you develop and extend the personality in your own players and not rely on merely copying an actor's performance back into the written word.

Neither can you successfully portray characters who are all good, or all bad; complexity in characters should never be undervalued, even in short story writing. Human nature being what it is, everyone is blessed with both negative and positive traits to their personality. If your villain is all bad, all you are doing is justifying his come-uppance in your own eyes. All of us have flaws or faults in our make-up and these should be honestly reflected in the characters we create.

People in real life are not drawn in black and white and neither should fictitious ones. Bishops may harbour murderous thoughts about the Dean; an international assassin may draw the line at destroying a work of art. A well-known film producer once told a writer that he could destroy his conception of a murderous hit-man with no conscience, just by having him stoop to stroke a cat on his way to the murder. Even Hitler loved his dog, Blondie.

Unless your novel is being written in the first person, the story needs to be multi-dimensional. That means checking out all your characters. Secondary performers must be given a life of their own, if they are to perform their proper function. The development of their role is as important as that of the main characters, or they will appear wooden, moving through the plot like cardboard cut-outs. You can't have one dominating set with everyone else scooting around on the periphery of the story. As with live theatre, the supporting cast should be there to *enhance* the role of the

102

leading players, not overshadowed by them. You can't give your main characters all the best lines to let the rest muddle along as best they can. The arch-master of the supporting role was Shakespeare, so take a look at how he managed to inject life/dialogue into his sundry players.

Margaret Finch uses astrology as a basis for plotting her characters. "Viewed objectively as a writer's tool, astrology can be invaluable as an aid to good characterisation, as well as being a certain cure for writers' block. Ruth Rendell uses this ploy in *The Lake of Darkness* and her principal character, a Scorpio, never once steps out of character. There are many facets to his nature, good as well as evil, but he is totally believable.

"Conversely, the 'heroine' of a romantic novel I once read was an irritating hotch-potch of several different people which made for a less than satisfying read. She had red hair and a fiery temper; was out-spoken and courageous, afraid of no man, and bent on vindicating her allegedly wronged father. A born fighter, a modern Amazon ... Yet every time the supposed 'villain' of the piece, i.e. the 'hero' spoke to her in a particularly high-handed or arrogant manner, she choked back/swallowed/was unable to stifle a sob. It just didn't ring true.

"Arians are so concerned with getting their own way that they have no time for such Piscean weakness. A cutting rejoinder would have been more in character. By the time she had changed into a typical Cancerian by cooking him a conciliatory *cordon bleu* meal (without even mixing toadstools with the mushrooms!) I had begun to lose patience with this tiresome little chameleon.

"Any astrologer will tell you that this conformity to one sign does not happen in real life. But for the purpose of clearly distinguishing one character from another and making them all credible, any popular sun-sign book, such as *Sun Signs* by Linda Goodman (Pan) which contains no technical jargon whatsoever, will put you on the right lines. It is very amusing, though perfectly authentic, and can be treated like any other writing reference book; the list of characteristics is in itself an inspiration for new ideas and can be a life saver when you're bogged down by writers' block.

"Racking my brains for original plots after breaking into the true confessions market some years ago, I experimented by putting up a chart for a date chosen at random. It would show any problems likely to be encountered by anyone born on that date which I could fictionalise. Two of them were enough to trigger off a story."

Sex ... Just how far should we go?

The majority of novels, regardless of genre, have some interaction between male and female principal characters - i.e romance and/or sex. Despite running the gauntlet of current political correctness, sex and violence are still marketable commodities but just how far should the fiction writer be expected to go in order to give the manuscript the right amount of reader appeal?

The sexy block-busters fall into two categories: On one side we have the Jilly Cooper variety that conjure up those delightful old fashioned words like 'risque' and 'ribald' rather than carnality. Cooper's sexual romps are merely 'jolly good fun' and like most things in life, should not be taken too seriously.

On the other hand we have the heaving, panting, groaning and sighing brigade who can't let a page turn without someone doing something to someone else's wife or husband. Recently, in an idle moment I picked up a paperback that promised to expose the secrets of Hollywood society and in a double page spread, nine people were committing some sexual indiscretion in six different locations. (I'll leave you to work out the logistics but I assure you it is possible.)

As Janie Jackson points out, the 'romantic' genre encompasses more than the standard boy meets girl story. "Do you favour glitz (Jackie Collins and Judith Krantz); stories of suffering (Danielle Steel); 'bodice rippers' (Rebecca Brandewyne); historical (Jean Plaidy and Philippa Gregory) or blockbusters (Sally Baeuman)? Study all these writers - and don't forget the 'greats' of the past such as Jane Austen and the Bronte sisters. Only then will you be sure of the type of romance you wish to write. The good news is that there is room for all and plenty of publishers are interested."

Hotting up the pace a little, the block-buster novels of around 200,000 words with an international flavour provide pure escapism for the reader. One thing you cannot avoid with this type of novel is the importance of sex or "weird sex (straight sex is too dull)," according to a *Daily Mail* researcher who had analysed more than 20 top-sellers. Nowadays sexual encounters need to have a gimmick and this has included lesbianism, bondage, homosexuality and incest within the recent best-sellers. The ideal examples for glizy novels comes from writers such as Barbara Taylor Bradford, Jeffrey Archer, Shirley Conran and Jilly Cooper.

Janie Jackson:
"Despite the jeers of the cynics, romantic novels always top the PLR lists. And if Mills & Boon publications were included in the Top Ten Best-sellers, they'd head that list, too. But many would-be writers imagine that romantic novels are easy to produce. All you need, they claim, is the 'formula' and large doses of sex. When these writers actually try to write romance, they swiftly discover that it is as demanding as any other form of writing.

Large doses of sex are not mandatory, either. If you build up strong sexual tension between your hero and heroine, explicit sex scenes may ruin the story. Several years ago I attended a talk given by Mills & Boon writer Stella Whitelaw, who had some good advice on the subject. "If you're no good at sex," she advised, "don't do it." Her remark brought the house down - but we all knew what she meant. Whenever I try to write steamy love scenes, I imagine my Mother glancing over my shoulder and saying "Really, dear ...!" As a result there is no explicit sex at all in either of my romantic novels - but they were accepted for publication."

In *Writing The Blockbuster Novel*, (Little Brown) novelist Albert Zuckerman informs the reader that novels about convicts, blue-collar workers, welfare recipients, Vietnam and the Cold War, showbiz, history, politics and 'coming of age' stories are all OUT while genetic engineering, computer technology, AIDS research, arms dealing, electronic toys and money laundering are IN.

Despite Mr Zuckerman's gloomy prediction, however, crime/thrillers are still top of the pile for the reading public.

A brief glace at the IN category will show that although publishers have moved away from war and spies (violence and explicit language in the traditional sense), subjects such arms dealing and money laundering would produce violence and vocabulary of a different nature. While an in-depth story on AIDS research would require a certain amount of explicit language and, possibly, violence, if the scenario included the street-level human interest of rent-boys and under-age runaways. Kept in context, the use of both adds authentic dimension to the characters and plot.

The majority of thrillers begin with the discovery of the body, preferably during the first chapter, and more often than not, making its appearance on the first page. A body is essential to a gripping plot for the simple reason that whereas most readers expect the murderer to get his come-uppance, they can be dreadfully fickle about fraud or robbery, particularly if the crime is so daring and ingenuous that the criminal deserves to get away with it and no one is hurt in the process. Therefore, the essential ingredient is a most original method and reason behind acquiring your body.

Possibly the most bizarre fictional killing I have ever come across was in *The Weight of the Evidence* by Michael Innes, in which the victim was squashed flat by a falling meteorite! The killer had worked out that weight x drop = impact and the somnolent victim had been murdered from above via the services of the said meteorite. Like sex, explicit language and violence is a personal thing, so don't think you have to use it in order to spice up the plot.

Writing For Children/Teenagers:

A small percentage of writers are interested in fiction for children and teenagers without realising this is also a highly specialised market-place. The first point to remember is that many of the books *we* enjoyed as children have since been labelled 'politically incorrect', so unless we have inside information about what publishers are currently looking for ...

Cass Jackson:
'"I thought I'd start by writing for children.' The speaker was a beginner writer and she was consulting us about how to get started. 'I suppose that's the easiest avenue?' she went on. 'Then when I get some stuff published in that field, I can go on to some real writing.' We swallowed our fury - after all, she was only voicing an extremely common misconception. How was she to know that writing for children/teenagers needs all the usual literary skills, plus a lot of special requirements?

If you aspire to become a successful children's writer there are a few questions you should ask yourself. Firstly, how much *contact* do you have with children/teenagers? Because publishers want 'stories about, and for, children of the nineties' - you must be able to meet children on their own level. Today's children are nothing like those of 20/30/50 years ago. Their lives are so full, their experiences so varied, that it's all too easy for a story to merit the contemptuous dismissal - Boring! Avoid cliched writing - believe it or not, publishers are still offered stories about buried treasure, secret passages and - worst of all, stories which end 'it was only a dream'.

Secondly, is your writing lively and original? If it's not, you have very little chance of succeeding. Children (like adults) want to read stories which take them out of their everyday lives into an exciting dream world. The stories, however, must be true-to-life and logical. It's a tall order but if you can do this, you will eventually succeed. Try to introduce a new twist which will add that vital touch of originality to your work, and above all, don't be tempted to re-tell stories from your own childhood. Avoid any hint of preaching or moralising; children/teenagers are quick to notice - and resent - this. Beware, too, of writing down to your reader.

If you really want to know what sort of stories teenagers like, a new publication from the Young Book Trust could provide the answer. *Our Choice 2* is an up-to-date review of more than 80 books selected and reviewed by teenagers - available from your local book store

Starting to Write a Novel: Bones & Padding

All novels start with a germ of an idea that slowly develops into something tangible and solid More often than not, the idea has been germinating in the back of your mind for years; characters which have been slowly aiding the development of the dialogue and plot, now clamour to be heard aloud. But, there is a vast gulf between starting a novel and finishing it.

In an article in the American *Writers' Digest*, author C. Stroy points out: "There's a talent part of writing and then there's the craft, and they're two different things. The talent comes in while conceptualizing a story; the craft is what lets you put it on paper in a coherent form."

The Bones:

So let your talent take care of the characterisation and plot. Firstly, in a card index, large notebook or on a word processor, set down the sequence of your story. The important thing is to have a clearly defined idea of where your story is going right from the start. There will be many cross-roads and U-turns along the way, even the odd dead-end, but this is all part of learning the novelist's craft. The important thing is to get all those messy notes and unrelated ideas *out of your head* and into some semblance of manageable order on paper or screen.

Secondly, define your principal characters using the same system. Describe their characteristics, personality defects, virtues, colouring, quirks and foibles. The basis for your story is knowing in advance what is eventually going to happen to them.

Thirdly, prepare an outline of the complete novel. You need to decide on a starting point - past, present or future - which will effectively and believably link up with the conclusion. Trying to make it up as you go along, doesn't work; you need to have a rough outline of when the events in the story are going to occur and in what sequence. Without this, it will all end in tears.

These three exercises are the bare bones of starting to write your novel. You may have your ending clearly mapped out but find at some later stage that the story has a different idea to the one in your outline. Don't be too hasty to disregard the messages because the unscheduled conclusion may turn out to be a more striking ending than the one you had intended. 'Gut-reaction' can be an important writer's aid; a side-shoot of talent which should be carefully nurtured.

An additional exercise in craftsmanship at this stage could also save hours of frustration once the novel is finished. Trying to decide how long the manuscript is going to be, is a bit like asking: 'How long is a serpent's tail?' But it's an important facet in 1990's novel writing.

Some publishing houses like Robert Hale will consider almost any fictional genre but there is a word restriction of 80,000 maximum on most. Mills & Boon often restrict their manuscripts to around 45/50,000 words. If your family saga is going to run to 150,000-200,000 words, including two world wars and up to the present day, you'll need to know which publishing houses are likely to consider accepting a potential block-buster of these proportions.

The best place to discover this information is the Public Library, so be prepared to spend a lot of time in there with a pad and calculator! A boring thought, I agree, but it could save considerable effort at the end when you're trying to cut or stretch your manuscript to fit the publisher's requirements. On the plus side, by having this information in advance it does mean that you can work out a balanced chapter outline before you start, because you have a definite framework within which to work, right from the beginning.

So now you have a chapter outline, details of your characters pinned up in front of you and a broad synopsis of where the story is going to lead. It's been estimated that any book will take at least 2,000 hours to write, so setting yourself a strict routine is essential. Don't worry if you haven't thought of a catchy title - the idea will come out of the blue and the last thing you want to waste time over at this stage, is what you're going to call it, since either you or the publisher will probably change it anyway. (None of my four completed manuscripts have been offered to publishers under their original working titles.)

It's also been said that the most difficult thing you'll ever write is the first line of your first novel - but even if you can't think of a punchy, riveting, gut-churning first line, press on with your narrative. Let the characters tell their own stories (where possible), through dialogue and action, whilst avoiding pages of high-blown purple prose - today's publisher's don't like it. And don't feel compelled to include every single detail about your location, characters and plot in the first chapter. You'll overload your reader with detail when what they want is action.

By using your chapter outline and synopsis it will be easier for you to keep track of the events shaping the plot. If you have room, use spread sheets pinned up on a board, and if you can't remember when the hero first confessed his impotence, a quick glance at your charts will put you back in gear without the need to flick back through dozens of pages.

Writing a novel is not an easy task; it's hard work, time consuming and at times, heart breaking but the thing that will always separate the amateur from the serious writer, is that the serious writer will finish the job. And having finished it, will re-assess it, re-write it where necessary and continue to learn from the mistakes. The serious writer accepts that the first completion is, in effect, only a first draft. Before s/he considers it good enough to send to a publisher, the author will have probably re-written parts of the text several times before feeling completely happy with it. Have you got that kind of stamina?

The Padding:
Writing the first draft of a novel is the easy part. You've off-loaded all the ideas and got the characters all going in the right direction; there have been a few unexpected developments but nothing you couldn't handle - *but it doesn't work*. There's something missing.

These flaws probably manifest themselves in what is sometimes referred to as 'the padding'. This is the element of the novel which adds depth and dimension to the story. This does not mean that pages of description can cure it; the solution is far more subtle than that. Firstly, look at the characters you've created. Are they *real* enough for the reader to empathise with their traumas and difficulties; their lives and loves?

Have you put too much emphasis on A's background, so that it becomes a total cop-out for decent feeling? Why are you, the author, justifying B's reaction to C, when you condemn D for a similar mistake? Is your story believable? Which brings us to the plot ... Have you explored everyone's motives? Nobody does anything without a reason, valid or not, so is there sufficient explanation for X's behaviour to Y? Or does it sound hollow and contrived?

Do you really care what happens to them? Because if *you* don't, how can you expect the reader to feel anything other than indifference? It is characterisation that moves the plot along and gets the reader believing in it; if it's not working then it's back to the drawing board, I'm afraid.

Long physical descriptions need careful pruning. If your heroine's eyes, instead of being 'liquid pools of sapphire blue' were replaced with 'compelling eyes that developed a slight squint whenever she was nervous or uncomfortable', you kill two paragraphs with one edit. Physical description should only be used to imply character and add a little depth to your story-telling. Today's readers are more interested in what goes on in a person's head, rather than being told how beautiful the heroine is, so cut the 'shimmering, long blonde hair' routine.

If you feel your characters have enough padding on their bones to make them real and compelling - what about the location of the action? Again, pages of descriptive prose will not necessarily give the right atmosphere to draw the reader into the story. A 500 word description of the herbaceous border can probably be replaced by the 'astringent, dew-sharpened scent of ... ' Lists of flora and fauna do not a novel make.

Also to be avoided is a Pickford's removal inventory of house contents. Again you cannot create atmosphere from a furnishings or arts catalogue; neither does estate agent's parlance pass for good scene setting. *Atmosphere* is the key word when it comes to location, rather than endless descriptive detail. If *you* can't see your location, how can you expect your reader to? Unless you're familiar with your subject, make sure you have sufficient reference books to hand to fill in the gaps, or take yourself off for a weekend's break to somewhere similar to what you have in mind.

These are, of course, hypothetical problems, but every first novel is subject to some (if not all) of them and every author who has ever written a novel has made the same errors in the early stages of their career, so you shouldn't be afraid to admit yours. There is a tremendous satisfaction in completing a novel but as with every form of saleable writing, you need to be much, much more than just a good writer. The secret is being your own sternest critic!

Too Long or Too Short:

Many writers believe that a story (long or short) finds its own length in the telling but Lewis Hosegood has a few tips of his own when it comes down to finally deciding on the natural length of a story.

Lewis Hosegood:

"Cutting - especially in the short story but also to a certain extent with the novel - it is essential to prune. We frequently need to condense in order to fit a required length; sometimes we have to cut ruthlessly, even if this goes against the grain of our natural preferences and susceptibilities. However, far from inhibiting our fine literary style we could find that cutting actually improves it. Pace is the important thing. In a novel this can, and indeed should, vary over the chapters, but in a short story it needs to accelerate all the time, the climax being its conclusion.

Here are a few suggestions for trimming an over-long story:
(1) Dispense with anything unnecessary. This sounds obvious, but what is necessary? Only that which sets the scene, promotes

the action, and activates the characters. The rest is ornament - though this too can play a part.

(2) Avoid over-description. Understatement, suggestion, is often more effective.

(3) Never repeat, unless for deliberate effect.

(4) Tighten sentences by shortening, especially in passages of tension.

(5) Use contractions wherever possible ('she'd' for 'she had', etc) not only in dialogue - it makes for speedier pace (in a short story anyhow).

(6) Make a dialogue racy and natural, perhaps by omitting the occasional pronoun, verbs, etc. as we do in real life conversation. For example: "He used to come and stay here once, I believe, or at least so they tell me. He absolutely loved the place. I think he used to call it his second home. That's what he declared in his letters, anyhow." Now this might be fine in a novel, but in a short story it could be better reduced to its essentials: "He used to stay here. Loved the place. Called it his second home."

(7) Avoid pedantic or old-fashioned words (like 'declared' in the above, when 'said' would do just as well), especially in dialogue.

(8) Omit inessential 'and', 'the', 'however', 'then' and occasionally implied verbs if the meaning is clear - even if again this results in (strictly speaking) non-literary language. "He glanced up the street. A delivery van on the corner. Nothing else." rather than: "He looked casually up and down the street. There was a delivery van of some sort on the extreme corner, otherwise there appeared to be nothing of great interest." We can break the rules of syntax when we can demonstrate we know them elsewhere! Anyhow the pace is more exciting.

9. Telescope phrases, e.g. 'All at once' to 'suddenly'. 'Now and again' to 'occasionally'.

10. Use other verbs to convey speech.
ie. "O.K," he said with a smiled. Could become "O.K." he smiled.

11. Don't sustain description for too long. Once the mood, setting or character is established (as succinctly as possible) forget it. Keep moving.
12. Avoid slack 'tell all' dialogue (the 'One lump or two?' slough of banalities). Remember: dialogue has three essential functions:
   (a) To pin-point and develop the character.
   (b) Further the action.
   (c) Usefully explain something previously unknown.
   Once any of these have been utilised there's no need to go on using the device. Sandwich it between narrative and vice versa.
13. Direct Speech is usually preferable to Indirect. "Wrong!" he said. Could be better than: 'He told her she was mistaken.'
14. Verbs are stronger than adverbs.
15. Choice of punctuation can help. Though nothing wrong with its use, the semicolon is more leisurely than the dash or the comma.

Some new writers, however, seem to suffer from the reverse difficulty. "I can say all I want in a short story of 500 words," they claim. "How can I make that into a 1500 word magazine story without padding?"

But they are probably just telling an anecdote, a bald outline of the plot, a mere synopsis. To give more body to such a story, I normally suggest they:

(1) Develop the character(s).
(2) Make description more realistic.
(3) Use cross-conflicts or mini-conflicts along the way before the climax.
(4) Make full use of suspense - tension, temporary relief, then more tension.
(5) Use dialogue to open up the story more.
(6) See the action in vivid scenes, then dramatise. Don't throw away opportunities. Seize them wherever you can.

114

(7) Intrigue the reader by fresh additions. Hint subtly at things to come. But make him wait.

(8) Put yourself in the place of each character. How would you react as that person? Then get it across convincingly and sympathetically.

But remember, every story has its natural length. A novel is a novel, and cannot be condensed. A short story which really works at 2,500 words is probably meant to wear that size. If it can't be re-worked to fit competition or editorial requirements, then write something else."

Preparing A Synopsis:

The art of writing a synopsis of a full-length book is almost as important as creating the complete text. The correct way to submit any full-length manuscript for consideration is by enclosing a detailed outline of the plot, together with the first two sample chapters - because for the targeted publisher, this will be the only indication he has of your capabilities as a potential author.

"Create the novel in miniature, although the synopsis should do more than merely summarise the plot," according to an article in the American publication, *Writer's Digest*, suggesting you should "use everything: action, description, exposition ... even dialogue to highlight dramatic moments. The object is to make the publisher feel as if he or she has read the whole novel." On the question of length, the *WD* states that, "Five pages is too short. Thirty pages is too long." UK publishers appear to settle for less by accepting two pages minimum/five pages maximum, but it's worth bearing this in mind for possible later submissions to American publishing houses.

As I've said before, never, never, send a complete manuscript to a publisher without first submitting a synopsis. *The Writer's Handbook* gives details of how to make an initial contact with each individual publishing house, so study the rules carefully before submittal. Since the American market is more geared to high profile selling, it is worth quoting another tip from *Writer's Digest*: "Some authors swear they get better responses when outlines (synopsis) are single-spaced rather than double spaced. The theory is this: When editors see a double spaced manuscript, they automatically pick up a pencil and look for things to change. A single-spaced outline, on the other hand, looks like a book! Editors read it less critically. Take your pick.   If you single space, leave one line of space between paragraphs. This will help your outline read faster". So pay attention to your synopsis. It's important.

Pseudonym:

If, like Janie Jackson, you can recognise that you have a problem in getting to grips with a style or subject that appears to be alien to your own character or personality (such as fantasy, erotica, horror, etc.,) try working under a pseudonym.

Ann Cook works under several different names and wonders if this change of identity turns a writer into a character of his/her own creation, part of a fictional world of our own invention. Of her pseudonym she says: "She is more daring than I could ever be ... Able to use the odd snippet of bad language without a twinge of conscience.   She's bold, flamboyant, inventive, imaginative, decisive, feminist and outspoken. I enjoy hiding behind her, since she lets me say the things the everyday me cannot. And very few people know who she really is, which is all part of the game!"

Leo Llewellyn also works under a different name. "A writer's name is important. It reflects our personality or our *alter idem*, our other self. This other self (or selves) remain hidden for most of the time, sometimes only surfacing when we sit down to write. There are actually three of me!

"Personality Number One is a day-to-day capable, amiable soul who is often taken advantage of because of a genuine desire to help. It produces a regular series of general readership articles and (usually) offends no one. It's a comfortable character with a sense of discipline who can dash off a 1000 word article by return of post when necessary!

"Unlike Personality Number Two who is flippant, brittle and apt to irritate for not taking matters seriously enough. It is genderless and can only produce material as a result of outside stimuli, i.e. people watching, a phrase in a magazine, etc.

"In complete contrast, Personality Number Three is dark, forceful and by nature, intensely esoteric. Although it doesn't suffer fools gladly, it's the sort you know would always stick around when everyone else had deserted. Of the three, this is the serious, ambitious writer."

There's a rather apt story about a now famous actress who, in her early days was unable to get the big break. A friend suggested she changed her name and after a considerable amount of deliberation, settled on one that conveyed the exact opposite of her usual pretty, soubrette image. Apparently, from the moment she "christened herself anew, a slumbering strength and power seemed to wake in her ... She seemed to be imbued with magnetism and filled with a set purpose."

A change of name is not going to bring over-night success but it might add a new dimension to your work or outlook. But be careful in your selection of a *nom de plume*, make sure it's one that sits easy on your shoulders and won't be a source of embarrassment in the future.

Finally, having finished one book, don't waste time sitting around waiting for the results - start on the next one. One tip given me very early on and it's one which I've repeated several times already: both agents and publishers are interested to know what else you have in the pipeline, and if you have other novels in the writing and planning stages, then you will be of more interest than a 'one-off' author, who may not be able to produce anything else.

Would-be authors should not be fooled into thinking that as soon as their book is accepted by a publishing house, financial rewards will follow. The Society of Authors are quick to point out that from the contracts seen by their legal department, more than 90% of publisher's advances are under £5,000 - many being in the hundreds rather than the thousands. It may also take another 18 months to two years before your book arrives on the bookshelves. So, where do the telephone number advances come from that the press are so fond of quoting? Answer: Probably out of the journalistic hat!

In an article printed some time ago in *The Sunday Times* on the subject of publishing advances, Melvyn Bragg admitted: "It is understandably impossible to get publishers or agents to reveal an author's advance. But although it may be an impertinence, there is no way that a comprehensive view of a book's publication can make much sense without it. Occasionally the author offered me the figure; more usually I checked around and came up with what I would claim to be reliable *guesstimates*."

Obviously there will be no large cash rewards for a first-timer and to quote from David Bolt's *An Author's Handbook* ... "It won't be paid over all at once; you will get half on signing the agreement and half on publication ... If the sum is indeed in the hundreds rather than the thousands, it won't be enough to retire on. Royalties are normally paid every six months and once your agent (if you have one) has deducted his 10-15%, your first excursion into the publishing world may well have cost you a great deal of personal expense."

If you still want to write fiction, begin by making a concerted effort to study as many different authors as possible in your chosen genre. The library will provide the novels (although government cut-backs now mean fewer new novels appeared on the shelves); haunt your second-hand book dealer for cut-price paperbacks. Small Press publications such as *Metropolitan, Tees Valley WRITER* and *Staple* set good standards for contemporary fiction, while *Acclaim* gives a reliable indication of what is happening at competition level.

Don't overlook the fiction slots on both national and local radio (including the *Talking Newspapers* for the blind and hospital radio), and the wide open field of writing drama for television. Producers are constantly on the lookout for new writers for situation comedies, drama series, soaps and one-off plays. Only when you begin to understand what today's editors, publishers and producers are looking for, will you be able to set your sights on the right target.

Recommended Reading:

The definitive how-to book on novel writing, *Write A Successful Novel* by Frederick E. Smith and Moe Sherrard-Smith (Escreet Publications) is now in its third printing. In one comprehensive, practical guide the authors provide the answers to over 200 questions would-be novelists want to ask about the writing of a novel and its successful marketing. ISBN 0-9517623-0-3

How To Write For Television by William Smethurst is a complete guide to writing and marketing television scripts. The author has written numerous scripts for both radio and television, been television script editor at BBC Pebble Mill and executive producer of drama serials for Central Television and is now director of an independent television company. Contains plenty of information and advice, together with illustrated examples. ISBN 1-85703-045-1

The Fiction Writers' Handbook. In her own inimitable fashion Nancy Smith informs us that publishers receive an average of 500 new novels every day from authors who are hoping to write a best-seller, although the majority do not understand the finer points of writing and submitting a manuscript. Drawing on 12 years experience as a creative writing tutor, she takes us through a checklist of essential fiction writing techniques for both novels and short stories; how to get published and rewriting in response to rejection. This is a short, sharp lesson in fiction writing and well worth investigating. ISBN 0-7499-1152-2

Chapter 6   Writing Non-fiction

The MORI poll also indicated that the most popular books with the reading public were non-fiction, read regularly by 24% of the population, while 19% of those polled enjoyed biographies. Further figures, given by the Policies Studies Institute, following their report on books, libraries and reading in *Cultural Trends* found that overall 60% of buyers bought reference books. Other non-fiction was bought by 36%.   A fair indication that non-fiction offers the widest market outlet for authors of full-length books.

Feature articles also make up the greater proportion of material used by national, professional, trade and special interest magazines. For every piece of fiction used in a magazine, there can be between 6-12 articles encompassing every aspect of social and/or technical interest.   Unfortunately, many writers do not understand the correct method of structuring feature articles and although most have a firm grasp of their subject, few know how to turn that information into saleable material.

The most common freelance mistakes are those found in:
(a)the historical/literary essays which, unless they happen to be linked to a local event or anniversary, are of no interest to the majority of editors;
(b) amateur offerings usually conspicuous by the lack of anecdotes, quotes, original material and/or human interest that often read as though most of the details have been lifted verbatim from a guide or text book;

(c) opinion pieces covering every subject imaginable, giving the freelance writer's view as paramount importance. Editors leave opinions to regular columnists.

Starting Small:

Learning to produce saleable fiction, ie. writing feature articles for the nationals requires that the beginner serves a vigorous apprenticeship before jumping in at the deep end. The competition is fierce and the standards demanded are often far higher than the new writer can often attain in the early stages of a writing career. Fortunately, there is an alternative as Graham Stevenson explains ...

Graham Stevenson:

"Many aspiring freelance writers harbour thoughts of having their work published in the national glossies and so target their writing accordingly. There is nothing wrong with this approach, of course, it is natural to desire a high degree of success. But the competition for such pickings is fierce. It is therefore inevitable that a great many who compete for them will be unsuccessful much of the time. There can be only so many winners. So doesn't it make sense to give yourself the best possible chance of scoring at least some success by aiming at less ambitious areas of writing as well? A great many are up for grabs each week and are relatively simple to conquer."

It was this market place Graham Stevenson explored in his book *How To Make Money Out Of Writing.* Just about every periodical and newspaper in print invites Readers' Letters; popular magazines such as *Chat, Reader's Digest, Private Eye, Take A Break, etc.,* use all manner of fillers from colourful quotes, word games and crosswords, household tips, recipes, poetry and humorous photographs - many pay between £5 and £25 for suitable material. And of course, while submitting fillers to magazines like these, the beginner is familiarising him/herself with editorial preferences for more ambitious submissions later on.

Graham Stevenson:

"As you can see, there are many opportunities to have your work published easily and quickly. And earn a little into the bargain. So it is a good idea to keep routing out the smaller markets just to keep up spirits while you struggle to crack the big time. The more you send out, the more chance you have of winning prizes. Just think how many that could be: in this chapter alone we have covered almost three thousand outlets annually!"

Another *Quartos* contributor found that becoming a 'village correspondent' for her local free newspaper gave her a good grounding for more specialised article writing. Having first made herself known in the area by contacting all the local schools, churches, community centres, clubs and sports groups, she was able to spread the word that the regular slots would provide free publicity for their social/fund raising events.

Of course the space available in the free newspapers is governed by the amount of advertising, "so be prepared to swallow your pride when one of your favourite pieces is shortened, or cut out altogether, to make way for an advertisement for the local garage," she warned. Even though the rewards are small (as low as 9p per line) you will still need to react to the undertaking in a reliable and professional manner, sending your copy regularly each week since the editor still has strict deadlines to meet and if your copy arrives late - someone else's work will appear instead.

Choosing The Right Approach:

There are all sorts of ways beginners can ease themselves into the turbulent waters of feature writing but it pays to chart in advance, the jagged rocks that lurk beneath the surface, ready to tear a hole in your carefully researched article. Week after week editors turn away well-written material on all manner of subjects and if your manuscripts are attracting only rejection slips there might be one very simple answer...

... You have still not learned how to look for the original slant or viewpoint that makes your particular piece stand out from the others. Christine Hall, author of *How To Be A Freelance Journalist*, having worked for newspapers, trade and consumer magazines both in the UK and abroad, offers her guidelines for successful feature writing. Since she understands only too well, the position of the overworked features editor, whose job it is to reject unsuitable manuscripts, her advice is invaluable for the beginner.

Christine Hall:

"You know you can write. Your features are well structured, thoroughly researched and topical, yet all they bring are rejection slips. What's wrong? Answer: You are probably approaching your feature from the wrong angle. Try this little test: What would you make from this information?

Back in the days of the steam railway, the Redhill Railway brought prosperity to Little Redhampton. In 1952, it was no longer considered profitable and closed down, despite protests from Little Redhampton's citizens. In 1990, Rosalind Roundmouth, retired schoolteacher from Little Redhampton, bought what was left of the tracks and grounds. A newly founded organisation, The Redhill Railway Revival Club, raised funds to contribute towards the purchasing price. Under the guidance of a retired car mechanic, the Redhill Railway Revival Club rebuilt the line between Little Redhampton and Darkoak Green, and restored the badly damaged engines. The railway opened in 1992 as a new tourist attraction. The interest from both locals and tourists has exceeded expectations by far. It appears that the new Redhill Railway is soon going to become a profitable enterprise. Its first anniversary is approaching.

Jot down all the feature ideas which come to your mind before you read on ... The possible ideas can be arranged in five main groups,

(1) The history of the Redhill Railway/Little Redhampton in the time of the Redhill Railway/The history of the steam railway, etc.

(2) Why it is important to revive Redhill Railway/Why we need more courageous citizens like Rosalind Roundmouth/ Why Redhill Railway never should have closed down/Why we have to preserve our local heritage.

(3) How the engines and carriages were restored/How to repair badly damaged historical engines/Technical difficulties in re-using old tracks/Case study of how one particular train was being restored.

(4) The business side of the enterprise/Promotion strategies for the Redhill Railway venture/Finance and calculation of the venture/How to make money by re-opening historical monuments and railways.

(5) A personality profile of initiator Rosalind Roundmouth/A personality profile of the car mechanic who was responsible for the restoration of the engines.

Now tick the group (or groups) of subjects to which your ideas belong. Then decide which you would write, BEFORE you continue reading ... Most freelance writers would go for 1 and 2. Most editors would go for 5! Some, depending on the type of publication, would select 3 or 4. This gap between supply and demand accounts for many rejections. As editors, we receive piles of submissions of 'The History of ...' and opinion features, for which we have little use. But we don't get enough material of the sort we really want."

[*How To Be A Freelance Journalist* - Christine Hall]

Even then it's not all plain sailing. One of our reasonably successful feature writers managed to chalk up an impressive collection of writers' gaffs, which he subsequently turned into a filler article for *Quartos Magazine*. Nevertheless the message came across loud and clear: Be careful not to offend against editors' scruples because this is more easily done than might be imagined. As our reader pointed out, no-one was likely to send an article on home-made wine to a temperance magazine, but he had heard of another writer who, despite having had several craft work items published in a Jewish magazine, queered his own pitch by sending them that article on home made Christmas cards.

Our reader wasn't a vegetarian, but he'd produced several saleable articles for vegetarian magazines both in the UK and America. When he submitted a further piece on throwing a children's party to *The Vegetarian*, the editor rejected it because the menu included jelly and ice cream, both of which normally contain animal products.

As already mentioned to illustrate the necessity of market research, he sent *The Countryman* a piece about an eccentric 19th century landowner, oblivious to the fact that the editor was opposed to blood sports. "Besides recounting some of his unusual habits, I mentioned that he was Master of Foxhounds, who had his huntsmen dressed in an unique livery and mounted exclusively on grey horses. The editor returned my article with the comment: "He seems to have been the sort of countryman who is best forgotten!'" The writer also submitted a manuscript to a rambler's magazine featuring the Wye Valley Walk, casually mentioning that a friend had completed the long distance walk in twenty three and a half hours - the terse rejection slip, admonished ... "The Association does not encourage walking for speed."

So what do editors want?

Christine Hall:

"**Personality profiles** based on interviews are always in demand. Bear in mind that quotes characterise a person better than description. Most beginners structure personality profiles like a c.v. in chronological order which tends to be boring.

(1) Begin with a short, succinct quote which characterises the person's attitude to his/her work.

(2) One sentence about the person - who is she?

(3) One sentence that quantifies his/her recent success with a precise, surprising figure (ie. 'one million records sold').

(4) One paragraph quote how s/he feels about this achievement, broken up by description of his/her appearance, gestures,

125

facial expression or tone of voice (ie. 'there is pride in her deep voice when she talks about ...').

(5) Continue alternating one or two paragraphs narration with one paragraph quote.

(6) End with a humorous quote.

The typical **subject feature** is of a specialist nature (ie. 'The role of Hungary as an export market for ice cream'), is often long and in-depth. Because of the wealth of information and the factual treatment, subject features tend to be boring. Do your best to liven them up with quotes.

(1) Begin with an introductory paragraph which may contain your by-line (ie. 'Amanda Scribble visited Hungary to investigate the country's market potential'.) This paragraph must contain a surprising fact, which is topical and of relevance to your feature, to hook the reader.

(2) The main text begins with a provoking quote from someone who is knowledgeable (perhaps the director of a company which exports ice cream to Hungary).

(3) Write two paragraphs explanation about the situation (why do so many western European producers target the Hungarian market? How much ice cream do Hungary's own factories produce?

(4) For the rest of the feature, alternate quote and narration. Use quotes from several people who represent different viewpoints (another British producer eager to export/anti-import pressure group/an Hungarian housewife/ice cream salesman). For narrative use hard facts (ie. 'The most popular flavours are chocolate, coffee and coconut'), backed up with figures (ie. 'total annual ice cream consumption is 1.7 litres per capita').

(5) Keep your own opinion out. Instead, finish with a quote from someone competent who sums up the situation in the way you think, and who can give a brief statement of what to expect for the future.

Many newspapers and magazines published in-depth **topical features** to provide background information to news articles. The difficulty is that you have to obtain controversial quotes, and compile and verify a huge amount of information within a short time. If you can, at the same time, give the feature a new angle and show the facts in a different light, you deserve a by-line in a national newspaper!

(1) Start with one or two sentences describing the fact as it is generally seen.

(2) One paragraph which shows the fact in a new light.

(3) One paragraph quote by someone who is competent and well-known and who sees the facts in this light.

(4) Two paragraphs analysing the background of the situation in more depth.

(5) One paragraph quotes from someone who holds a different opinion (probably your first contact's competitor or opponent, or the 'villain').

(6) One paragraph quoting your first contact, contradicting what the second person said.

(7) One paragraph narration.

(8) One paragraph from a third person, such as the woman in the street.

(9) Continue by alternating one or two paragraphs narration, one paragraph quote.

(10) End with a paragraph which gives a summary and a critical (but not patronising or moralising) future outlook.

The **How-To feature** is easy to write as well as easy to sell. DIY and 'how to save money' subjects are particularly in demand. However, you must be an expert, i.e. you must have done it yourself.

(1) One introductory paragraph which motivates the reader.

(2) Between three and twelve bullet points (or up to 20 numbered paragraphs) of between one and two sentences. Arrange them in chronological order.

(3) The last paragraph refers to costs or gives an address for further information.

Opinion features are the most popular category among beginner writers, but the least popular among editors! There are hardly any commercial outlets for opinion features, unless you are a VIP expert in your field. However, you can try writing an 'Opinion piece' for *New Woman*, or a comment column for your club or society's newsletter. Last but not least, the structuring recipe for opinion features is suitable for a reader's letter. If you want to see it published, avoid the typical beginner's approach (opening with a well-known fact, proverb, or question) - this will read like a school essay! Avoid a patronising tone.

(1) Start with a surprising fact, if possible relevant to the season, or to a topical event, and develop your thoughts from there.

(2) Alternate two sentences thoughts, two sentences facts throughout the feature. This makes your article easily readable. Quote a couple of precise figures and state the source; they make you appear competent.

(3) Finish with a question, related to the future."

The amateur writer is overly fond of submitting anecdotal humour which, more often than not, refers to some domestic/ family crisis. This rarely appeals to an editor for the simple reason that it fails to amuse, but non-fiction workshops reveal that this is a popular writing style among beginners. Take for example this small extract from a feature article by Lucy Hawking (daughter of the famous Professor) which appeared in *The Daily Telegraph* ...

"Once a stray scientist was so over-awed at reaching the home of his idol that he fell into the rose bush by the front door. It became tangled with his string vest, and he had to be cut free with the kitchen scissors."

This highly visual and amusing incident was confined to a mere 44 words - an amateur would have milked it for all it was worth and stretched it to around 800 words by introducing every trivial domestic detail that sprang to mind while the writing was in progress.

Another approach least favoured by editors, is the article written in the first person. Unfortunately most beginners seem to feel the uncontrollable urge to intersperse their articles with 'I' regardless of the subject. The plain truth of the matter is that no one, particularly an editor, cares what *you* think about a subject. An expert writing about a subject can sometimes utilise first person singular because s/he is writing from personal experience but as a general rule of thumb, leave 'I' out of it.

As Shirley Read observed: "Regular columnists in the Press can get away with the first person singular. Often their brief is to chat the readers amusingly through 'their week'. Sometimes a very gifted feature writer can manage it because he or she has that natural knack of turning the most ordinary, mundane event into a chucklesome anecdote. There is also the celebrity who comes along with an interesting first-person story. But humbler writers like you and me should think twice before submitting an 'I' piece. Fascinating as it might be for us to put down on paper an incident or experience in our lives, but in all probability, no editor will share our enthusiasm.

This does not mean, of course, that you cannot draw on personal experiences to use as subject material for articles as Bernard Towler found to his advantage. "An article packed with those three words 'I', 'Me' and 'My' is probably unsaleable - but you can write about people, happenings and places you know, in ways which will bring enjoyment to the readers."

By drawing on his own career in the N.H.S, our writer sold several articles to the *Funeral Service Journal* (aimed at funeral directors and their staff), including a piece entitled 'My First Funeral' chronicling his own grandmother's funeral which had taken place 50 years before. His working background also provided a piece for *Purchasing & Supply Management* which told the story of over 30 years health service purchasing in the N.H.S.

Who To Write For:

Perhaps the widest and most diverse outlet for freelance writers are the county, country and regional interest publications which invite articles on wildlife, different aspects of country living, superstition, nostalgia, regional cooking, local crafts, folklore, legends, country sporting events ... Sentimentality should be avoided at all costs and also the patronising tone that often manifests itself in articles from 'country converts'.

Do bear in mind that readers of publications such as *Country Life, The Countryman, The Lady, Heritage, The Field, This England, Evergreen, etc.,* are experts on country-living and will not tolerate inaccurate, amateur scribblings in their favourite publication.

Most counties have their own magazines which feature almost anything related to activities/interests within the county boundaries. Study a few back issues before approaching the editor with any ideas you may have, since you may be repeating articles run in previous issues. The library edition of *Willing's Press Guide* will furnish you with the initial editorial contact information.

The second largest market place must surely be the hobbyist magazines that cater for a wide range of sports, hobbies, collecting, crafts, etc. Needless to say, the writer needs a certain degree of expertise before attempting such outlets and it's also important to gauge the degree of competence required from the contributors by studying past issues.

For example, there are some eight regular equestrian publications but the editor of *Pony*, a magazine for 10-16 year olds, would not be interested in the same type of material published by *Horse & Hound*.

The following examples are only a small selection of national, wide circulation hobbyist publications listed in *1000 Markets for Freelance Writers*, that will consider unsolicited submissions. Virtually every hobby/sport has a publication devoted to that specific interest and it is doubtful whether any writer could go through *1000 Markets For Freelance Writers* and not come up with at least one magazine for which they could write an article. See how many of the listed interests are covered by members of your family ...

Sport:

Clay Shooting; Rugby; Running: Cricket World; Cycling Weekly; Bowlers World; Bowls; Hockey Digest International; Boxing Monthly; The British Archer; Martial Arts Today; Amateur Golf; Angler's Mail; Angling Times; Boat Angler; Darts Player; Athletics Weekly; Fast Car Magazine; Fighters; Football Management; Autosport; Bodybuilding Monthly; Women & Golf, etc.,

Pets/Animals:

Cat World (offers opportunities for freelance material but according to the editor, 'everyone wants to write about their cats'); *Dogs Monthly; Cage & Aviary Birds; Wild About Animals; British Horse; Budgerigar World; Birdkeeper; Birdwatch Monthly, Aquarist & Pondkeeper,* etc.

Hobbies:

Amateur Gardening (will consider freelance submissions but like all the rest, the writer is advised to write in with one or two suggestions carefully targeted at the regular reader); *Boat International; Buying Cameras; Film Review; Gamesmaster; Gardeners' World; Camcorder User; Home & Studio Recording; Homebrew Supplier; Keyboard Player; Camping & Caravanning; Sound on Sound; Canal & Riverboat; Rambling Today; British Chess Magazine; Ballroom Dancing Times; Amateur Photography; Climber & Hill Walker; Practical Boat Owner; Astronomy Now; DIY Week,* etc.,

Collecting:

Medal News; Military Hobbies; Model & Collectors Mart; Antique & New Art; The Antique Collector; The Antiques Dealer & Collector's Guide; Art Monthly; Stamp Magazine; Book & Magazine Collector; Map Collector; Treasure Hunting; CD Classic; Record Collector; Coin News; The Collector; BBC Music Magazine, etc.,

Crafts

The Clockmaker; Scale Aircraft Modelling; Dolls House & Miniature Scene; Crafts: Good Woodworking; Embroidery; Needlecraft; Popular Crafts; Knitting International; Practical Woodworking; Routing, etc.,

In addition to sports and hobbies, there are also vast selections of technical or professional magazines which will accept material from freelance writers. Some years ago a colleague of mine spent sometime working for a foreign manufacturer of wood preservative as a publicity consultant and as a result, turned out a nice profitable side-line in producing technical articles for trade publications such as *The Timber Trades Journal* and *The Architect's Journal.* She had no first-hand working knowledge of wood preservative but she did have access to the right people and the relevant technical data, so was able to turn the material into saleable features.

Similarly, *Sound On Sound* is a practical hi-tech music magazine concerned with serious music recording and studio equipment. Nevertheless, this did not stop an amateur musician, who happened to be a qualified electrician, submitting an article on the most effective way of soldering connection wires for electronic music equipment. Another two-way approach was illustrated by a hi-tech feature on electronic keyboards and synthesizers for a magazine similar to *Sound On Sound,* which was re-written for a computer magazine to show what minimum equipment was actually required to produce electronic music for computer programmes.

Alison Whitehead also found out that you don't need specialist experience of a relevant trade to be able to write for that market. "During the time spent as a care assistant in an old people's home, I went through several different uniforms, some of which were better than others.

"Later, when I began to explore the trade press in general, I stumbled across *Corporate Clothing & Textile Care*, which deals with all aspects of business uniforms. I immediately thought that the assistant's uniforms might possibly of interest to the readership. It didn't take long to map out my idea and send it to the editor ... I sold the article for a very useful fee."

A Simple Exercise:

To illustrate how many different magazine permutations there are in selling an article, try this simple exercise with a topic of your own choice. Let us say, for example, that a writer has a certain amount of expertise with indoor/house plants - for a slightly different viewpoint she decides to slant the piece to feature 'Designing With Plants'. The feature needs to explain which plants grow best under different conditions and environments; which are selected for texture, colour and shape; when to use artificial plants; care and maintenance, etc.,

The obvious first choice for market outlets would be the ten most popular (1) gardening magazines listed in *The Writer's Handbook*. Since most of these publications have a house plant section, the first draft article will probably be targeted at one of them. Where else would you think of 'designing with plants'? Possibly the second choice would be the (2) home interest magazines which include the monthly glossies. Third choice (3) women's interest publications that offer all sorts of opportunities for 'designing with plants' - herbs in hanging baskets, air plants for bathrooms, brightening up a bedsit with hanging baskets ...

... and the ideas do not stop there. Who else would use plants to brighten up a public area? There are magazines aimed at (4) architects & planners; (5) shops & offices; (6) hotels & catering; - (7) hospitals and clinics often use plants in reception areas - so why not a more technical feature on plants for poor environments, coupled with care and maintenance? Employers are always looking towards improving the working environment which suggests another outlet with (8) trade & business management publications as well as (9) marketing & public relations and (10) exhibition & conference industries.

One subject x ten different categories probably gives you in the region of 100 magazines as a possible outlet for 'Designing With Plants'. Of course, the article that appeals to the teenager trying to brighten up a basement bedsit will not be the same one that catches the eye of the architect who is looking for ideas for the multi-million £££ office development in the City. Each new outlet needs to be thoroughly researched and copies of the relevant magazines obtained to ensure your writing style is tailored for that particular publication. (This is where *Willing's Press Guide* comes into its own.)

'Indoor Plants' was a subject chosen at random by a non-writer for the purpose of this exercise - but it illustrates just how extensive the scope is for good article writing. So far we have seen how important it is to find the right target or angle, but even good ideas may not stand up on their own - you still need a gimmick, hook or eye-catching title according to **Christine Hall**:

" ... and if you switch to the following subject areas, your number of acceptances may multiply immediately:

Human interest stories/Personality profiles:
Each time you read a news article or hear about an interesting event, ask yourself: who is the person behind this? Why did they do it? How did they achieve it? What obstacles did they have to overcome? What effects does this event have on their lives? Interview them, and base your feature on this interview. Personalities need not be famous, but they have to be interesting. Don't structure a personality profile like a c.v. - concentrate on recent and current events. Remember that quotes characterise a person better than descriptions.

Features on Royalty:
With a bit of thought you'll come up with feature ideas that can be linked to Royalty. When I was offered a feature about a local artist who'd been commissioned to paint the Queen's racehorses, I accepted immediately. The writer was a beginner - but she certainly had journalistic instinct!

Anything to do with sex:
Sex in the headlines helps sell a publication. Find a respectable way of including the subject in your feature, which suits the style of the publication. When I was editing the business magazine *European Frozen Food Buyer*, I published a feature on 'Sexy advertising campaign for ice cream in the UK - will producers in other countries follow the example?' A survey among subscribers showed that this was the most read feature of the issue.

Money & how-to pieces:
Every editor welcomes original articles on how to save money. Domestic hints, how to earn money (from turning a hobby into a profitable sideline), or how to find/keep a job. You may find it hard to believe but editors don't get enough of these feature categories. Instead we are drowning in piles of opinion and historical pieces, which are nicely written, but useless."

Study your target publications, and start collecting ideas how you could slant any of the above suggestions to fit those particular markets. As Christine Hall explained, providing your approach is professional (e.g. analysing the market, careful research, query letter before submission, use of quotes, journalistic style and proper presentation), the number of acceptances and cheques will soon exceed that of rejection slips.

Other twists to the personality profile or human interest feature are the opportunities for autobiographical material. Although straight forward biographies can be difficult to sell, if the event or person can be linked to a local happening or national anniversary, it might help you towards an acceptance. In *Writing Your Life Story*, Nancy Smith not only shows how to record a family history but how to produce a readable autobiography with commercial overtones. Working on the premise that readers are more interested in people than things, Nancy fully realises that publishable material needs a few 'fictional techniques to add colour to your story' and explores the full potential of re-writing extracts as saleable articles.

Nancy Smith:
"But for those who feel daunted by the idea of tackling an entire book, why not start with short, article-length pieces? Simpler to write and easier to sell, they can be expanded and incorporated into a book, if you wish, later on.

Personal experience articles are sought by many different markets and include travel and anything with a topical slant, such as an important anniversary. This is where you must not forget to study the market to ensure you send the right material to the right place. A useful, saleable length for these short pieces is around 800 words, though, obviously, that depends on which market you are aiming at."

Be realistic, however, about your biographical material. Recently a writer approached a tutor at a writers' workshop to enquire where she should submit two dozen volumes of a family journal, consisting solely of modern domestic letters dating from the 1980s. *The Pastons* it wasn't, and the writer was highly miffed when the tutor suggested the high street Prontoprint service for copying and binding. The extract submitted for assessment was totally uninteresting, badly written and poorly presented. It may have been of immense interest to the family concerned, but a publisher would have rejected without a second glance.

Feature writers should not overlook local radio for possible non-fiction outlets as Tricia Gerrish found when she approached the producer with an idea for 'two or three features on life in Devon, seen through the eyes of an 'Incomer' (using the local name for new arrivals). *Reflections of a Devon Incomer* ran for 20 episodes and while she took a break to consider an angle for a second series, Tricia was able to adapt ten episodes for publication to coincide with the start of the next series.

"The experience of writing to length, meeting deadlines without compromising quality, and recognising the germ of an article in the smallest hint will have been invaluable. Add to these the exhilaration of being a published author, confidence to seek success in other markets and occasional requests to talk on my experiences, I also have a wordprocessor earned with carefully hoarded fees."

Going For Gold!

Sooner or later, the freelance features writer is going to want to tackle a full-length book using the mountain of research material and interviews that have provided all the information for dozens of those published articles. But it's not as simple as that; full-length books aren't made up from a series of separate articles. It's not enough to be enthusiastic about your subject and to have amassed enough research material to sink a battleship; you must have either unearthed previously unpublished facts to act as an addition or counter-argument to popular theory, or discovered a new slant to a subject that hasn't been written about before.

So it's back to researching the markets to discover where your non-fiction book could fit into a publisher's current list. *The British Library Cataloguing in Publication Data* should provide a list of books in the same subject index and a visit to a large Public Library will be worth your while, to find out what exactly is available for the researcher. Do bear in mind that many reference books will no longer be in print for a variety of reasons, but libraries do not discard those no longer in publishers' catalogues and often, your local library is the only place where you can track down essential reference works. If you are unsure whether a book is still in print, ask your local bookseller to check with *Whitaker's Bookbank*. (W. H. Smith use their own reference system which is not as extensive as *Whitakers*.)

Obviously if you've been writing about a particular subject for some time, you will already have access to expert testimony, or at least know whom to approach for essential quotes, etc. Initial discussions with your 'experts' might even help to pre-define the interest level at which you will aim your writing. If looking at the student/beginner/amateur, there is little point in over-loading the book with unfamiliar jargon; conversely you must not talk down to your readership - they will obviously have a smattering of interest to have picked up your book in the first place. Strike the happy medium by using more familiar terms, in such a way that the text gives the meaning without painstaking explanation.

Just like the fiction manuscript, each chapter should pass smoothly from one to the other, covering each aspect of the subject as it arises; and if you find there is an important passage which won't fit into the text without spoiling the flow, stick it in the appendix with a cross reference! Just as the novelist needs to make sure that the action and characterisation is maintained throughout the story, so too, must the non-fiction writer pay attention to the drama of knowing the exact moment to introduce his newly researched material. If this is introduced too early, the reader finishes the book with a sense of disappointment and frustration.

By a general rule of thumb, the non-fiction book still needs a beginning, a middle and an end. Phase One: The beginning normally introduces the topic under discussion; makes reference to previously published material on the subject including both for and opposing viewpoints; and introduces the reason behind the writing of a new book. Phase Two: Introduces the new in-depth research/discovery and brings in generous quotes from previously *unpublished* sources. But don't be tempted to use all your surprises just yet. Phase Three: Draw together all the loose strands and arguments, saving one or two surprises until the very end. Non-fiction should still finish with a bang, not a whimper!

Interesting a publisher in a non-fiction manuscript differs little from trying to sell him a novel. He will still require a synopsis outlining the basic 'plot' of the book, together with some background information on your qualification to write it. If you've managed to 'scoop' a well-known or prestigious expert to bolster your testimony, then make sure you milk the connection for all it's worth. Courtesy, of course, demands that you ask your 'expert' if it is permissible to name-drop for the benefit of selling your book to a publisher or agent.

Several of our contributors have found that there is a great potential in writing How-To books because whatever the subject, there is always someone who wants to know how to do something. If you have specialist knowledge then it could be to your advantage to turn it into a non-fiction book. The majority of creative writing books recommended as further reading in *From An Editor's Desk* have been produced as off-shoots from other writing interests.

Graham Stevenson:
"Many people have a specialist interest in life and are always eager to learn more about it. Hobbyists, for example, are constantly on the look-out for new techniques and advances in technology designed to help them. Sometimes, too, people have to acquire

some new know-ledge because of the force of circumstances. A daughter's unexpected engagement as the result of a whirlwind romance, perhaps, makes her father think fast. How does one arrange a wedding? What is the best way to go about organising a reception? Who normally pays for what?

Sought-after information is valuable; it sells books. If you can find a need for knowledge and can write a book to fulfil that need, you will make a sale. How-To books should be designed to save the reader time and effort of research. By bringing together the essential hard-to-track-down facts on your subject into one volume, you are bound to please your reader.

It is doubtful you will think of something completely new - just about every subject under the sun has been covered at some time, somewhere. If you can find an unique subject, fine - exploit it to the full, but if you can't, don't worry. Simply research out a new slant to your chosen subject. When I came up with the idea for *How To Make Money Out Of Writing* for example, I was convinced I'd thought of a brand new approach to the face of freelance writing and how to profit from it. Books on freelance writing are not new, of course, there are many of them, but mine held a different slant from the rest in that it concentrated on where to find the easiest markets."

But, as Graham is quick to point out, thinking of a subject and the way it is to be angled is one thing: writing it up successfully is quite another. Writing How-To books means you have a know-ledge of the subject and if it is to have a ring of truth it must be written from experience. Authoritative writing is likely to be sale-able writing - which also applies to feature articles. Facts are the life-blood of a How-To book and must always be accurate. One tiny slip and you will lose credibility and your reader's enthusiasm for your work will falter.

This rule also applies when considering writing for professional magazines, and as one reader pointed out, the payment for an article is the same, no matter who writes it, so it might as well be you! In this instance the writer was a social worker, specialising in working with the elderly; by collecting as many articles about her area of social work, together with magazines on residential care, management in social work departments, as well as 'in-house' social work magazines which were normally distributed free to social service departments and hospitals, she built up an impressive data bank of material. She also canvassed ideas from colleagues about things that annoyed or disturbed them, as well as making notes of anecdotes.

In writing for any professional or specialist publications, the basic rules are the same - although most would have an 'educational aspect', it is important not to talk down to the readership. You will antagonise the reader and provoke some 'extremely caustic comments' in the form of a 'Letter to the Editor', bringing ridicule to the author and a possible loss of outlet for future material. When quoting statistics, check with the library if you are unsure of the facts. Never, estimate because there is always someone willing to write in with the correct one.

The 'jargon' used in such articles also matters a great deal to an editor and outsiders or amateurs attempting to write for specialist publications would be spotted at once because there is usually a specific 'language' that only comes with years of experience within the given subject.

As with feature writing for the general interest magazines, professional publications also use anecdotes to illustrate specific problems or case histories, but do make sure that none of your subjects can be identified, unless you have their written permission to use the material verbatim. As our reader concluded: "If you are an experienced worker in your field, then you are sure to have something interesting to say."

Iris Bryce had been a freelance writer for nearly thirty years when she and her husband sold up their farm and went to live on a canal boat. This original lifestyle provided her with dozens of ideas for a book and although it took some time to discover the right theme or angle, *Canals Are My Home* caught the public's imagination.

The success of this book was followed by *Canals Are My Life* and

140

Canals Are My World. But the subject was far from exhausted as Iris went on to explain.

Iris Bryce:
"By now I was writing articles for a magazine allied to the waterways, and after a while I added a few recipes; the editor liked them and so I started a cookery column 'Cooking On A Boat' ... I eventually published a small cookbook myself, *Canal Boat Cookery* ... and although never having done this before, I had 1000 printed and sold them all in the next 15 months - mostly by going around the shops myself."

The appeal of Iris Bryce's books can obviously be found in the diversity of her material. Despite publishing four books on the same subject, she has consciously steered clear of repeating stories from previous volumes and made an effort to ensure that each one, whilst retaining her own distinct style of writing, has a fresh approach to offer the reader. The waterways of England have provided her with three non-fiction books, a self-published success with the off-shoot cookery book and numerous articles - she wonders whether the waterways will continue to provide enough background material for her children's stories and fiction.

Plagiarism & Copyright:

It is the writers of non-fiction who most often come up against the question of using quotations from other authors' books and the infringement of copyright. Each year in the up-dated edition of *The Writer's Handbook,* Editor Barry Turner includes an article on the current discussions and alterations to the Copyright Act, though as from 1995 the terms of copyright will be decided by European law. By regularly up-dating your own copy of *The Writer's Handbook,* you will at least ensure that there are no hidden surprises when it comes to using someone else's text.

In the 1993 edition, Barry Turner discussed what was considered to be 'fair dealing' by organisations such as The Society of Authors and The Publisher's Association. As he rightly pointed out, it is not the done thing to lift 'a substantial part' of a copyright work without permission but unfortunately there is little agreement on what constitutes 'a substantial part'. 'Fair dealing' is usually considered to be the use of a single extract of up to 400 words, or a series of extracts (of which none exceed 300 words) to a total of 800 words from a prose work, or of extracts to a total of 40 lines from a poem, provided that this does not exceed a quarter of the poem.

If you intend to use a 'substantial' extract from another author's work, however short, courtesy demands that permission be sought from the author, or publisher of the original work. And don't leave it to the last minute, warned Barry Turner: "It is much in the author's interest to deal with permission as early as possible. Last minute requests just before the book goes to press can lead to embarrassing difficulties if the fees charged are too high, or if permission is refused."

Recommended Reading:

Writing Your Life Story by Nancy Smith (Piatkus) is a step-by-step guide to writing your autobiography, whether you're planning a full-length book or a shorter article. This book is aimed at those who had thought about writing their life story but felt that it was too enormous a task. The author discusses newspaper and magazine articles using the same material and gives advice on how to make submissions to editors. ISBN: 0-7499-1361-45

Journalism for Beginners by Joan Clayton (Piatkus) gets down to the real nitty-gritty of writing for the nationals and what is more important, offers a series of exercises aimed at those who are seriously interested in the professional approach. As Ms Clayton points out, opportunities for journalists are far greater than those for short story writers, since publications print at least four times as much non-fiction as fiction. There are valuable tips that go against much of what is generally taught by writing tutors. For example: Did you know that a justified right-hand margin is the mark of an amateur in an editor's eyes? Or that a sentence should never be more than 27 words long? ISBN: 0-7499-1188-3

Interviewing for Journalists also by Joan Clayton (Piatkus) draws on her experience as a full-time journalist writing for several national newspapers and major women's magazines. Every journalist needs to know how to interview people for profiles and news features because quotes add interest and authority. This book will show you how to develop and polish your interviewing skills, find and talk to the right people and get the information you need. Packed with practical advice and exercises, you will learn how to research your subject, approach members of the public, celebrities, politicians, specialists and even royalty. ISBN: 0-7499-1350-9

Writing Feature Articles by Brendan Hennessy (Focal Press)is now in second edition and offers detailed instruction to both the budding journalist and the aspiring freelance writer on the techniques required for writing feature articles for newspapers and magazines. The author is a journalist and lecturer who has written feature articles for many newspapers and magazines from *The Times, The Guardian* and the *Daily Telegraph* to *Country Life* and *The Radio Times.* ISBN: 0 7506 08846.

In *How To Make Money Out Of Writing* (Gower), Graham Stevenson examines the market where the beginner could look for a first success and to gain confidence in his or her own writing abilities. Maintaining that almost everyone can write saleable short material or 'fillers' for magazines if they know how to go about it, this book sets out to guide beginner writers towards the easier markets and simpler forms of writing, so that they can see their work published in the shortest possible time. *How To Make Money Out Of Writing* takes the beginner through the stages of what to write, formulating ideas, research, presentation and recognising the market for fillers. ISBN 0-7045-0630-0

Chapter 7 Writing Poetry

Poetry always stimulates heated discussion so I decided to open this chapter using two rather controversial quotations. The first observation from a most unexpected source - "A poem is a series of words so arranged that the combination of meaning, rhythm and rime (sic) produces the definitely magical effect of exalting the soul to divine ecstasy." - comes from Aleister Crowley (wearing his poet's hat) and aptly demonstrates the elitist viewpoint that poetry is more than mere words.

The much simpler quotation taken from Rudyard Kipling - 'And the first rude sketch that the world had seen was a joy to his mighty heart/Till the devil whispered behind the leaves,/ "It's pretty, but is it Art?"' - sums up the patronising, artistic snobbery often used by traditionalists when referring to the writing of modern or contemporary poetry. (An opinion frequently echoed by classicists when referring to contemporary orchestral composers.)

Poetry is, unfortunately, the most controversial area of creative writing since there is the continual and continuing debate over what is, and what is not, a good poem. Traditionalist die-hards claim that if it doesn't rhyme it's not poetry, while modernists believe that anything goes. Some editors will print just about anything to keep their readers happy, while others are so selective that their choice is almost inaccessible to the general reader.

Poetry stirs the savage breast rather than soothes it, and heaven help the editor whose selections fail to please the readership. More vitriol has been thrown in the face of convention in the cause of poetry than any other art form.

In order to confuse the issue still further, there are literally hundreds of small press poetry and literary magazines which regularly use poetry, but even an in-depth study of them all would provide no satisfactory conclusions as to what can be classed as 'good' modern poetry. There is a world of difference between the quality and quantity of the material involved and each publication is supported by a dedicated bunch of *aficionados* who maintain that their's is the only true, enlightened approach to poetic expression. We can only reach one sensible conclusion: ***Poetry, like music, is very much a matter of personal taste.***

So why is there so much elitism attached to poetry in comparison with other forms of creative writing? What do poetry editors and established poets advise? How should today's poet learn his or her craft? For the answers, we turned to Peter Finch who is, undoubtedly, one of the most important figures on the UK poetry scene - plus co-editors of the prestigious *Staple Magazine*, Bob Windsor and Don Measham.

Peter Finch:

"There is no money in poetry so rewards come in other forms. There are too many poets in too many ponds - most of them small. It's also hard to define success since national success is rare and local success common. The elite hold on hard to what they (think) they've won."

Don Measham:

"The paradox is that everyone thinks they can write poetry. It may even be a soft option: children often prefer to have a crack at poetry rather than other types of writing - because starting a new line (pausing for breath) is a more intuitive matter than prose punctuation. *Reading* poetry is another matter. If contemporary poetry is regarded as only for an elite who are anyway seen as only pretending to understand it, the reasons will include the following:
1) Most primary school teachers never read poetry of any kind.
2) The media has little time for it - except doggerel - other than in (elitist) arts programmes.
3) The oral tradition has shifted to pop, so that poetry has become

the business of 'lit crit'. In this milieu a poem may gain prestige because its obscurity leads itself to exegesis.
4) Immediacy is not necessarily sought therefore. Pop and advertising have stolen the rhythms that most modern poets are afraid to use.
5) Concentrated, precise, particular (i.e.. not ready-made) language is discouraged by the prevailing culture"

For many years, *Quartos* published very little poetry, with the exception of previously published material which had appeared in other magazines.   This, our editorial 'cop-out' informed the readership, gave a fair indication of what other editors were currently accepting for their own individual magazines. Listed in *The Writer's Handbook,* however, as 'the best single source of information on poetry competitions', it was rapidly becoming obvious that we needed to seriously consider including a showcase for contemporary poets on a regular basis.   Our difficulty was in deciding which style and type of poetry would compliment *Quartos* and it's practical 'nuts-and-bolts' approach to creative writing.

The problem eventually provided its own solution following the 1994 Open Competition when Abi Hughes-Edwards came up with some scathing, but justified, observations when compiling her judge's report after reading the entire entry. Although her original remarks were aimed at competition entrants, she has since found to her cost, poets too, in general, insist on ignoring editorial guidelines.   Presentation is as important when submitting a single poem as it is for any other typescript - and just as frequently ignored.

Abi Hughes-Edwards:
"I find an alarming repetition of certain pit-falls, not just the single terrible poem, but promising poems that suddenly reproduced the view from the pit-bottom. So though I am aware that it is often easier to criticise than create, I feel sufficiently moved to mention the following little reminders to some, trail blazers to others.

The first point seems so obvious that I blush to mention it. Please read the entry/editorial requirements and then fulfil them. Remember, an envelope, antique effect parchment, scented notelets, scraps and exercise books or any other myriad surfaces on which people write their poetry, *are not A4 size white paper.* The suitably inscribed skin of a close relative I may find personally enjoyable, but if it isn't within the entry/editorial requirements then you will be rejected. It may also be as well to remember that paperclips or, in some masochistic instances, staples are preferred, not pins; they draw blood and may unreasonably prejudice your chances.

Some say that poets cannot count. Rubbish; it is only the thrill of submission that makes some forget their counting skills and submit 60 lines for a 40 line criteria. Others compensate by writing their exact lineage in a very professional manner but there are extremes of compensation, and some of the more pedantic list the number of words, illuminate the capital letters and adorn their punctuation with slivers of gold leaf. It's not necessary.

Worst of all are those who, having written their poem, fear its being misunderstood and enclose an annotated appendix or large portions of a Slavic dictionary to aid translation. You may think I am exaggerating ... I'm not!"

Finding Your Target Magazine:

The message about market research applies equally as strongly to the poet as it does to the fiction or feature writer - and is just a frequently ignored! It is not uncommon for an editor to receive an envelope full of photocopied, single and multiple-page poems that obviously represent a life-time's work, with no covering letter or s.a.e. - and which have obviously been sent without any reference to the editorial guidelines or even a glance at a back issue of the magazine. The most frequent offenders with regard to the mega-submissions are those sending work from overseas.

Selecting a magazine from one of the many writers' publications with a pin does not give you license to bombard the editor with the entire contents of your desk drawer. Even new magazines have a definite idea of the type of material they will be using, so unless you can obtain an advance copy of the guidelines, wait until the first issue has appeared before submitting. By sheer token of the fact that he edits (or, in most cases, *owns*) a magazine, the editor is only going to publish what he likes and the only way to discover what that particular editor likes, is to study some back issues. The sole beneficiary from random and multiple submissions is the Post Office!

Understanding Poetry:

As Peter Finch pointed out in his article 'The Rise & Rise of Poetry' (*The Writer's Handbook 1995*), most people still do not read poetry and have 'not looked at a scrap since they were at school'. If the only entire piece we can recall to mind is *Skimbleshanks, The Railway Cat*, we are hardly in a position to understand or proffer an opinion on poetry in the 1990's. The majority of school-age children are deprived of an early introduction to the various forms of traditional poetry and it is not until much later, when they attempt to compose poems themselves, that they run into the problems of not understanding the technical structuring of poetry.

In an earlier chapter we discussed the importance of fiction writers familiarising themselves with the antecedents of their chosen genre; the same should apply to the aspiring poet in that, a familiarity with the different traditional forms can provide a valuable framework in which to create his/her own individual style. This is not to say that beginners need to plough their way through the epic poems of Ovid (even though they are immensely entertaining) in order to acquire a good grounding in poetry appreciation.

Bob Windsor:

"Go back to basics: read or listen to the Border Ballads, such as *Edward* or *The Twa Corbies* and look for the way a mystery is set up and its solution 'suggested' (not stated!). Also, similarly, the old English riddles in, say, *The Oxford Book of Nursery Rhymes*. Then read some pre-modern poets: Thomas Hardy, Walt Whitman, Gerard

Manly Hopkins, Wilfred Owen ... then get a mixed anthology of English verse, such as the Pan *New Golden Treasury*: do not read the moderns in isolation from what has gone before."

One concise introduction is *The Poet's Manual & Rhyming Dictionary* by Frances Stillman which will define in some detail many of the esoteric terms that crop up so often in poetry judge's reports and anthologies. This particular writer's tool has a threefold purpose,. It is, a) a reference book listing the styles and terminology, b) an overall view from basic traditional meters through to contemporary developments, and c) a rhyming dictionary to help find the elusive rather than the obvious.

The Poet's Manual explores the differences between epic (*Iliad, Odyssey, Paradise Lost, Beowulf* dealing with subjects on a grand scale) and narrative poetry (*The Idylls of the King, The Canterbury Tales*). The latter on a more human scale and includes ballads. Also examined are dramatic, descriptive and lyric poetry; satirical, occasional, light and humorous verse with examples to illustrate the differences.

If you follow this accessible crash-course in finding your way around rhythm and meter, free verse and the comparisons between modernist-traditional forms, you will go a long way in preventing the mistakes so common amongst new poets. In the chapters dealing with the content and style of poetry, the author has examined and clarified the development of poetic subjects and themes, as well as giving examples of the increasingly popular Japanese tradition in haiku and tanka. At the end of the day, however, you must realise that the final selection will be governed by an editor's personal preferences.

Abi Hughes-Edwards:

"It is very important that whoever is reading your work gets a sense, a feel of what you are trying to convey. I am not saying that poems should be reduced to a simplistic narrative form; poetry should experiment and challenge, but what I do dislike reading is the outpouring of an arrogant inner eye that refuses to share its vision.

Neither do I want to lecture on the structure of a poem. The profitable side of poetry does that in numerous books, pamphlets and no doubt by now, video! However, I do come across quite a few examples of the 'one line poem'. This is a poem in which the preceding lines or verse are of no consequence and serve as mere vehicles to accommodate a single idea, climax or rhyme.

These are frustrating poems to read; you can almost hear the poet saying: "I'll stick that in as it gives me the rhyme for that brilliant line I thought of earlier." The worst are those written for the last line; it makes one hell of a long read. Finally, almost every competition judge or poetry editor mentions free verse, so I won't - much - except to remind some that free verse is not an excuse to ramble tediously across a perfectly good piece of paper."

A D-I-Y Poetry Course:

This same, no nonsense approach is continued by Alison Chisholm in *A Practical Poetry Course*. Although a how-to book from the Allison & Busby stable, the whole text is structured in a series of 'poetry days' - eleven in all, which offer the aspiring poet a highly inexpensive writing course in an easy-to-follow style. The course approaches the craft and practice of poetry from six directions:

1) Exploring contemporary and classical poetry,
2) Getting the words down on paper,
3) Examining the administrative side of writing,
4) Learning how to enjoy the craft,
5) The study of new and traditional forms,
6) Developing and moulding poetry for publication.

Each 'day' concludes with a series of practical exercises which encourage original thought and instruction on how to find your way around the market-place. When you consider the cost of a poetry correspondence course this book can provide an extremely good alternative, especially as Ms Chisholm's poetry course is included in the Writers' College syllabus!

What do Editors Want?:

The only way to discover what a poetry editor *really* wants is to study several back issues of the publication. If there is no sign of rose-tinted Nature and pet cats, then you would be ill advised to submit something in this vein; conversely if the choice favours the nostalgia and sentimentality of Patience Strong, the demise of the occupants of Wacco, Texas (*a la* Lawrence Ferlinghetti) will not be well received.

In his latest book, *The Poetry Business*, Peter Finch provides a rather disturbing view from the poetry editor's desk, based on his days as a magazine editor. There are, we are given to understand, some who don't bother to actually read the submissions and accept work from 'known' poets on the premise that all the work submitted is good. Others, he writes, 'enlist a whole democracy of sub-editors which can subsequently guarantee that anything that is vaguely individualistic is rejected'.

Most, according to Peter Finch, compromise and read only the first page of any batch of poems, or sometimes even only the first few lines. "How else do you manage to get through upwards of 20,000 hopeful bits of verse a year? And believe me, for a successful magazine that figure is not untypical," he concluded.

Don Measham:

"Editors look for linguistic freshness, precision and strength of feeling without sentimentality. A sense of sound. Strong imagery, and sensitivity to the effect of the words used on the thoughtful reader."

Abi Hughes-Edwards:

"In looking look for publishable work from both established and new poets which will titillate the discerning reader, I wish to forestall two frequently expressed comments:

a) "It's not worth sending work in, it would just get lost under piles of pending poems." Wrong, good work always surfaces.

b) "I don't know what this wretched editor wants, apart from blood." I can't speak for anyone else, but this editor is like the King of the Copper Mountain, a character from a children's book who needed to hear exciting stories to keep his heart beating. By exciting, I do not mean poetry that grafts the body of Geena Davis onto the pace of Indiana Jones. What I look for in a poem is originality, ideas and images that make me respond and are, most importantly, clearly expressed."

Peter Finch:
"Evidence of an original approach; a broad and adventurous use of language; willingness to look at new forms and style. Also evidence of wide reading."

Abi-Hughes-Edwards:
"I will publish poems in any form; sonnets, villanelles, ballads - whatever, providing they are good. But I will not appease the appetites of those who crave boys on burning decks clutching Mary's little lamb, whilst celebrating the relief of some colonial outpost.

Similarly, appearing with sufficient regularity for me to comment upon are poems enthusing on the Christian experience. I am fairly tolerant of most non-violent forms of worship, but tend to be irritated by visions of a heaven made of clouds ruled over by a God that requires his subjects to suffer. Before 'Uplifted' of Cheltenham rushes to pen more verses on punishment and the blasphemer, may I say that although all poems are read, I am more inclined to look benevolently on religious poetry if it is approaching the standard of Gerard Manly Hopkins, rather than Randal & Hopkirk (deceased)."

Original Thought:
Whilst it is generally accepted that there is no such thing as an original thought, this should not prevent poets from trying to approach their chosen themes from a slightly different angle. Here we go back to the advice given in Chapter 3, of discarding the first

152

thing that springs to mind and look for a second, third or fourth idea that might be more exciting. Like all forms of creative writing, the poetry editor is looking for something thrilling and different.

Don Measham:

"Read, listen, look. Keep a notebook - write down a phrase or an observation when you don't feel like writing. Look at it later. Let the poem speak for itself. Don't go beyond having a hunch what the poem 'means' until you've written it. Sharpen the poem but don't add an explanation. If you find you've got one already, consider cutting it."

Abi Hughes-Edwards:

"It is possible to treat a common theme in an original manner; a sunset for example, a subject portrayed by many. One can always write about it from different aspects: BE the sunset, what it touches, how it influences, its absence, your loss, etc. Or try writing in a different form, a ballad or sonnet perhaps. Whatever you do don't just write lists of colours. Dulux do that already. The same may be applied to another poet's favourite - the seasons. Why should something as potentially wonderful as the seasons be reduced to a list of climatic conditions? The Met. Office does that; a poet should do more.

Of course death is fascinating. Our mortality is constantly with us, but to quote Mr Elliot: "I had not thought that death had undone so many." At least a quarter of the poems received are concerned, obsessed and turned on by life's great departure. Whilst understanding that bereavement and its accompanying emotions often provoke people to put pen to paper, I am always unprepared for such a donation of dead. Fathers, mothers, lovers and cats are the most written about, closely followed by children already deceased and children alive, happily playing in the garden whilst parent speculates on how they'll feel if offspring dies.

Some of these poems are really good, and need to be to stand out against so many, but others are merely therapeutic, the writing as inert as the subject. Again, original slants on the subject stand out, well written poignant epitaphs may start me sniffing, but some of the irreverent partnerships with death are far more enjoyable."

Don Measham:
"What to avoid - cliche, sentimentality, preciousness and fashionable tricks!"

Peter Finch:
"Cliche, tiredness, old byways, familiar clothes, seagulls, tramps, patinas, worn out forms. Editors want bright, new work."

Abi Hughes-Edwards:
"There are the few, of course, who can still turn themes such as carnally obsessed killer zombies from outer space into an experience marginally less interesting than sailing porridge skin from one side of the bowl to the other. The problem I see with a lot of poems in this category is *pace*, or rather, lack of it. The structure is turgid, the language laboured. If a poem is supposed to be exciting, one cannot just rely on the subject. Yes, playing with dynamite is stimulating, but only when it is dropped, thrown, inserted, etc., the language and structure must also thrill."

Where Are the Outlets?

Poetry has seen an upsurge of interest in the past couple of years and by 1995, Waterstones (self-styled 'leading poetry book-seller') announced that their 86 branches had seen a sales increase of 25% for new verse. Their marketing figures for poetry came to a staggering £1.75 million a year - roughly the same figure as that for hardback fiction. But is this reason enough for poets to get excited?

To provide the annually updated poetry input for *The Writer's Handbook*, Peter Finch needs to have his finger on the pulse of current publishing policy, both in the nationals and the small presses. Poems now have regular spaces in the up-market newspapers, although as he is quick to point out: "Poetry may well be selling better but its titles do not get into the top ten. *The Guardian's* annual list of the best-selling one hundred paperbacks featured not one collection of verse."

Among the mainstream publishers, a few do continue to produce slim volumes of new poetry but the competition is fierce. The new poet is advised to update his/her copy of *The Writer's Handbook* each year in order to keep as up-to-date as possible with the changing trends and editorial re-shuffles. This user-friendly guide is often the poet's first introduction to the small press titles which is a virulent breeding ground for new poets and poetry news.

Peter Finch:

"Small press publications sell to new and often non-traditional markets, rarely finding space on bookshop shelves where they are regarded as unshiftable nuisances. Instead they circulate from hand to hand among friends at poetry readings, creative writing classes, literary functions, via subscriptions, and are liberally exchanged amongst all those concerned."

Nevertheless he is quick to point out that numerically the small presses and the little magazines are the largest publishers of new poetry, both in terms of range and total sales (see Chapter 9). Each year the listings in the *WH* are revised and extended in order to increase the range and scope of poetry outlets. There are over 200 currently listed and hundreds more in the *Small Presses & Little Magazines of the UK & Ireland* (Oriel Bookshop). Discussions at the writers' workshops, however, indicate that even the more experienced writers are unaware of the vast numbers of market outlets for poetry - and an even greater number refuse to believe that they need to familiarise themselves with individual editor's preferences if they want to market their work successfully.

Another problem, of course, is cost. Having discovered the dozens of suitable poetry magazines, acquiring a sample issue of each is going to cost between £2.00-£5.00 per publication and very few of us have the sort of money which enables us to indulge in this sort of market research. Even writers' circles would find their funds rapidly diminishing if they were to order copies of every literary magazine that may, or may not, be of interest to their members. Local libraries may carry a copy of a regional or local press poetry publication but the poet needs to spread his nets over a much wider area.

Fortunately, there is an alternative central reference source which carries details and examples of the types of poetry being written and published today. Although based at the Royal Festival Hall (South Bank) in London, I can report through experience that out-of-town enquiries are promptly and efficiently handled by the staff at **The Poetry Library.** Next time you're in the capital, allow yourself a half day to browse around.

The Poetry Library houses a collection of over 45,000 titles of modern poetry published since 1912. The poetry of all English speaking countries is represented, including translations into English by contemporary poets. It houses a wide range of magazines and periodicals from all over the world and also has an audio collection of poetry on cassette, record and video which may be listened to on the premises.

The Library runs an information service which compiles lists of poetry magazines, publishers, bookshops, groups and workshops - all of which are available from the Library on receipt of a large s.a.e. It also has a notice board for 'lost quotations', through which it tries to identify lines of fragments of poetry which have been sent in by other readers. I've sent in several enquiries and they haven't disappointed me, yet.

All books are shelved in a democratic alphabetical order and all poets, however minor, are represented. It has always been the policy to keep two copies of each title as far as possible, with one available for loan and one permanently kept in the reference collection. The Library opening hours are probably the best of any public library in the country - it is open every day of the week from 11.00am to 8.00pm. Membership is free and open to all on the production of proof of identity and a permanent address. Members can borrow a maximum of four books for up to four weeks at a time. Postal and telephone enquiries are also very welcome.

Payment:

Despite the up-surge in popularity over the past few years, poetry's financial profile hasn't increased at all. "Its practitioners have been photographed by *Vogue*, decked out in Armani shirts, Versace jackets and Zegna suits. Faber have put Larkin and even the venerable Auden on t-shirts but poetry is, in reality, an unprofitable activity," is Peter Finch's message.

But it *is* one dear to the novice's heart, because general discussion time at writers' workshops always raises the question about which magazines pay for poetry? The answer: Very few.

You may find you are paid the odd pound or two from the financially established magazines but a payment of between £10-£40 is fewer and further between. More often than not you will receive a couple of complimentary copies and as Peter Finch pointed out in 'The Rise & Rise of Poetry', you can earn more money writing about it, lecturing on it, or by giving public readings. "In fact most things in the poetry business will earn better money than the verse itself. Expect to spend a lot on stamps and a fair bit on sample copies. Most of the time all you'll get in return is used envelopes."

Don Measham:

"Those who don't pay are either commercially more hard-nosed than we are - or fractionally more hard up. But, generally, those magazines which are in receipt of subsidy, should build payment to writers into their application for funding. The purpose of subsidy should be (i) dissemination, (ii) spreading what little money there is thinly. Most small press payments are, of course, only token ones but they are important if they help a recipient to regard him/herself as a professional - and work accordingly at the craft."

In his 1996 entry for the *WH* ('Poetry Has to be Easier than Working'), Peter Finch looked back over the year which had given us National Poetry Day, poetry on the Internet, poetry in the daily newspapers, poetry on television and radio. "Poets are everywhere," he tells us. "Keep looking and you'll find a slot."

Last Minute Advice:

Peter Finch:
"If it still sounds odd after several re-writes, then junk it. Don't waste time on dead things .. abandon it. Go out and read someone new. Start again elsewhere."

Bob Windsor:
"Roughly speaking, when writing prose cross out the beginning; with poetry, cross out the end. Always bear in mind that poetry is a compressed, evocative form of language. Keep it short. Cross out what's superfluous. Develop a keen ear for cliche and ready-made phrases. Before a cliche is abandoned, though, consider bringing it to life, e.g. Robert Lowell converted 'the daily grind' into what a dentist does."

Abi Hughes-Edwards:
"One tip I find useful when I've laid down my fountain pen is to leave, time permitting, a finished poem for a week, then go back to it. It's a rare poem that can't be tightened, and it can also work the other way; something you were unhappy with (perhaps as a result of over working it), can seem much better a week later when you are feeling more positive. It's putting into practice the old adage: "Absence makes the heart grow fonder"."

Lastly, if in doubt about a poem, try reading it aloud. At a recent writer's workshop the discussion came around to the winning poem in the *Quartos* Open Competition which had been published in the magazine. Several participants said that they neither liked nor understood it since it had been written without punctuation or capital letters to break up the text, i.e. it wasn't easy to follow. By coincidence a member of the group had attended one of Peter Finch's performance poetry evenings and allowed herself to be persuaded to read the unfamiliar poem as a performance piece. The breathless delivery of a small child visiting grandma's outside lavatory after dark, listening apprehensively to the scratching and rustlings of night noises, until the safety of the house was regained, was a first class rendering. It became extremely visual - it made the poem come alive.

The comments following the reading reflected the general opinion of the group: "Why wasn't it written like that?" It was - it was just that traditional thinking about poetry couldn't come to terms with something that didn't *look* familiar.

As Bob Windsor, co-editor of *Staple Magazine* explained earlier, contemporary poetry should not be isolated from traditional forms. Like contemporary orchestral music, it may be an acquired taste and like it or not, it is what the editors of leading poetry magazines like *Rialto*, *Staple* and *Envoi* want to receive.

Recommended Reading:

Writing poetry is a creative and imaginative process, but getting it published is a very practical one. *How To Publish Your Poetry* by Peter Finch (Allison & Busby) is a clear and detailed guide on how to get your poetry into print - for both the novice and the more established poet. ISBN 0 85031-631-6

The Poetry Business by Peter Finch (Seren) In his own inimitable style, Peter Finch, takes the reader through the tangled and esoteric world of publishing poetry with its pitfalls (many) and its rewards (few). Here he explores all aspects of writing, performing and publishing poetry in a witty and accessible style, peppering the facts and figures with anecdotes about the great and the good. A highly entertaining way of finding your way around this poetry business. ISBN: 1-85411-107-8

A Practical Poetry Course by Alison Chisholm (Allison & Busby) is arranged in a series of poetry 'days' and is laid out in a practical, easy-to-follow style of exercises. With over 400 poems published in magazines, anthologies and collections, she has also written the poetry course for the Writers College and *The Craft of Writing Poetry* in the same series. ISBN 0-7490-0114-3

The Poets Manual & Rhyming Dictionary by Frances Stillman (Thames & Hudson) is still considered by some to be the definitive writers' tool for poets. Designed as a reference book in the 'field of prosody' or the handling of language in poetry, it enables the poet to improve his writing by understanding the tradition and technicalities of his art. ISBN 0-500-27030-9

Chapter 8   Writing For Competitions

The subject of whether writers should enter writing competitions is a long running debate, with some even questioning the merits of supporting such hit-and-miss events.   One small press newsletter calculated that even after taking into account the prize money, adjudicator's fees and administrative costs, competitions provided 'a nice little money spinner' for the organisers. Although the newsletter was basing its calculations on the receipt of some 2000/5000 entries, many of the popular competitions fall far short of this sort of figure - between 200 and 600 appears to be the average number of entries received.

When the question was thrown open to *Quartos* readers, we came up with a good cross-section of responses but most came out in favour.   One reader said she entered competitions because she enjoyed the challenge and if she won a prize, it was a bonus; if she didn't, she made any necessary alterations after reading the published judges' report or the winners anthology, ready for entry in another event.   She recommended the exercise because another advantage of competition lies in the fact that both winners and runners-up are more likely to get themselves published.

Another reader with an opposing viewpoint didn't feel that the hit-and-miss method of submitting short stories for competitions could be recommended due to the lack of opportunity for any sound market research. Since a thorough market study couldn't be undertaken for competitions, he contended that an entry could only be submitted purely on speculation, and the chance of winning a prize was less than the prospect of a story written for a specific magazine being accepted for publication.

From the poet's point of view, yet another regular competitor considered competitions to be the life blood of a poet, since few magazines pay for poetry accepted for publication. "Competitions do pay," he added, "and provided you enter smaller, rather than the bigger ones, and go for the sort of organisation/judges who like the sort of poems you produce, then you do have a chance of earning some cash."

On a personal level, I previously held a suspicion that competition results depended on which side of the bed the judge got out of, on the morning of selection. These sentiments were echoed by Beryl Williams after the results of the first *Quartos* Open Competition were published. The winning story concerned the suicide of a war correspondent, having witnessed one battle-front too many. The second and third prizes were also awarded to 'darker' pieces and Beryl wanted to know: "Did nobody send in a story with a laugh in it? As most women's magazines ask for an 'up-beat' ending, did you not have any entries finishing at least with hope?"

Having organised five annual competitions for *Quartos* (and acted as a judge for several others), I now have a more sympathetic understanding about the process of selecting those often surprising finalists. The competition referred to above had been an 'open' event, which meant that there was no fixed theme, attracting a wide variety of entries. For the first competition the preliminary selection was made by a panel, with the final choice being that of the chairman of the local writers' circle.

Since this particular adjudicator wrote for publications such as *The Countryman* and *Window On Wales*, we were all greatly surprised when the first prize was awarded to that rather grim war story. What was inescapable was this particular entry was a powerful piece of writing, well constructed and original in the telling; quality of writing transcended a personal taste in theme. It also serves to illustrate that unfashionable/unpopular commercial themes, which currently have few market outlets, can come out top in competition.

This example also deflates the argument that if judges are named prior to the event, prospective competitors can steal a march on the others, by closely studying the writings of that particular individual. As John Copley drily observed: "If you happen to learn beforehand that the judge is keen on the Regency period then the temptation is to give it a whirl. Even doing this can backfire though. For all you know, every other competitor has had the same idea. The poor old chap may well become heartily sick of hearing about Fat Boy George after reading the twentieth such epic, and choose a story about Eskimo seal-hunters solely because of its (to him) sheer novelty."

Since organisers usually reserve the right to change adjudicators without notice, competitors can also have another problem to contend with, as Beryl Williams pointed out: "If you've entered a science fiction story for judge Isaac Asimov, and then find he's been changed for Barbara Cartland - hard luck!"

The second *Quartos* Open Competition had a set theme of writing for a country or county publication, and called for a poem, short story or article reflecting the taste of rural editors. In this instance the winning short story was a romance, couched in the form of a series of 'Letters To The Editor', which persisted until the writer, a shy retiring spinster netted the editor of a country magazine. Using the same process of selection, the prize was awarded for the original interpretation and sly humour contained in the piece, which appealed to both male and female panellists.

So in answer to Beryl Williams' question as to what should she be writing for her next competition entry ... "Shall I make it a funny one? Or will a story about death and destruction be taken more seriously as an art form, and so more likely be chosen as a winner?" ... there is no real answer.

Open competitions are exactly that: open events in which all styles and subjects compete for the prizes - although domestic stories with a 'women's magazine' slant are rarely selected as prize winners. Continuing on a darker note - according to the organiser of the Swanage annual poetry competition, Lewis Hosegood, humorous poetry doesn't find favour with judges either!

Following The Rules:

Despite the rules being clearly set out on the entry form, it is surprising just how many entrants refuse to work within the parameters set by the organisers. Many short story competitions receive entries which are not really stories at all; they are better described as commentaries or reflections on life. Never exceed the stated word count because if your entry is found to be 100 words too long, you will be disqualified - and it will be your own fault if you lose your entry fee. If the organisers have set a theme for the competition - stick to it. The selectors are instructed to look for the best interpretation of that theme and if you've ignored it, you won't be in the running, no matter how good your entry.

One localised short story competition discovered that half of the stories for their set theme failed to observe the requirement of the principle setting being that of a small harbour town. The judges' comments: "For the harbour town to be relevant, it should not be possible to be able to substitute 'crows over the church tower' for 'gulls over the harbour' without seriously affecting the story!"

Likewise, it is not advisable to take a manuscript from your stock-pile, alter a word or sentence to fit the theme, and send it off, hoping for a winner. Another competition stated that the story should have a 'foreign' flavour; one entry had the heroine 'crossing the *Place de la Concorde* on her way to work' - there was not one other word, phrase or description in the entire manuscript that had any reference to the fact that the story had a Parisian setting. Of course it is possible to restructure a piece to fit a given theme, but it takes considerably more thought than merely altering a word here and there.

The secret of all creative writing is originality but it never ceases to amaze competition judges just how banal some story-telling or poetry can be. The *Quartos* regular readers' competition usually has a set theme with a handful of suggestions to get the creative juices flowing. In one instance the given theme was 'a flower' - the editorial suggestions included the 'stone carvings on an ancient tomb; a rare, exotic blossom or a humble meadow flower; one that had been pressed between the pages of a book; a bouquet from an anonymous admirer or a funeral tribute'. The result: over half the entries featured a rose and were called - *The Rose* - the first thing that had sprung to mind.

One competition rule that does need some clarification was posed by the disqualification of the winning entry in a national competition. The rules for most competitions usually state that entries must be ... "original, unpublished and not entered for any current competition" - it was subsequently discovered that the winning entry in this particular event had been selected previously as the winner in a writers' group competition and the poem published in the groups' newsletter. It was, understandably, thought that inclusion in a private newsletter did not count as having been 'previously published' but as far as competitions are concerned, any work appearing in printed form, no matter how modest, should be considered as 'published' - especially when it comes to competitions where large cash prizes are at stake. If in doubt, make a note on the title page that the poem has appeared in a private newsletter or raise the question with the organisers in advance. Believe me, if you don't point it out, someone else will!

Presentation & Submission:

Every year, competition entrants waste hundreds of pounds in fees because they do not abide by the rules set out by the organisers. There are, however, dozens of other little niggles that can make a judge's or organiser's life hell when the entries start to come in. The following comments come from those involved in sorting, administering and judging national writing competitions.

The Bridport Prize: One of the most professionally organised events is the annual competition organised by the Bridport Arts Centre, and I'm grateful to Competition Secretary, Peggy Chapman-Andrews for allowing me to use their competition to illustrate how they cope with between 8,000-10,000 entries every year. The Conditions of Entry are clearly set out, for past experience has taught the Bridport organisers to list every possible permutation to cover the vagaries of entries submitted for the competition.

There are the usual rules and instructions governing the awarding of prizes and presentation. The rules stipulate that the pages of a story should be clearly numbered and securely fastened together, and should carry the title next to each page number. Since the manuscripts themselves should bear no names, addresses, or any other identifying marks, it is easy to see that entries not bearing the title next to the page number could easily be mislaid if the Arts Centre's cat should decide to assist with the selection process.

The Bridport organisers insist on an official entry form and failure to comply with any of the conditions could result in disqualification (at least 200 entries are disqualified every year just for breaking the anonymity rule). Imagine the chaos of 10,000 unidentified, untitled, unnumbered, unsecured manuscripts and you have a Competition Secretary's worst nightmare!

The adjudicators for the Bridport events are well-known literary figures who subsequently produce a concise report which is sent to all Bridport competitors who have enclosed a stamped addressed envelope for the purpose. This enables entrants to compare the comments with the winning entries included in the yearly anthology against their own submissions. Several of the larger competitions also publish a detailed report and an anthology of winning entries, which at least give an idea of the standard of entries required, but no one can give accurate advice on the subjects most likely to appeal to a selection panel.

Despite the rules set out clearly for each competition, Peggy Chapman-Andrews still found enough 'Do's and Don't's' to produce a full-length article for *Quartos Magazine*.

"My first piece of advice is a basic one - (a) read the rules, and (b) having read them, abide by them. The rules of each competition vary and we all have our own reasons for wanting things done in a particular way, so be sure you are obeying the instructions set out in the conditions of entry. For instance, if the rules tell you not to put your name on the entry itself, then it is sheer folly to write your full names and address on every page of a short story, or even put 'Joe Bloggs' after the title. That way you are heading straight for disqualification.

It never ceases to amaze me that writers of short stories send them in without fastening the pages together. Sometimes I have even had three or four manuscripts submitted by one author without any form of fastening whatsoever, and it has taken several minutes to separate and clip the pages of each story together. Some organisers might not bother, and the authors would only have themselves to blame for the ensuing chaos.

Do fasten together all the pages of each story, and fasten them securely; it is so easy for them to fall apart, however neat and tidy they may be when you put them in the envelope. If you must use those coloured plastic slide binders, do staple the pages as well. The binders may look very nice, but often come adrift before they are out of the envelope, and I have yet to see one that survives the rigours of being passed through the many hands that deal with it in competition.

If the organisers want two or more copies of an entry they will say so. If they do not request them, then only send one: they don't want to be cluttered up with copies they do not need, and it would be far better to keep the second copy for yourself. When submitting more than one poem, give each one a separate sheet of paper. If the rules limit the length of a story or poem it is no earthly good sending in one twice as long - that way, too, you are heading straight for disqualification.

Folding a story or poem in half to fit an envelope is acceptable, but do not fold them half a dozen times and force them into altogether inadequate envelopes. By the time they arrive they look distinctly tatty. If you must use computer paper, do separate it, then clip the pages together. Maybe it's just that I'm not computer minded, but for me it is very difficult to find the beginning and the end, let alone the middle, of a story that unfolds rather like a toilet roll in one continuous length. Talking of which, please do use typing paper for your entry and not toilet paper!

When enclosing a stamped addressed envelope for your entry to be returned (and not all competitions return entries), do be sure it is big enough to take the manuscript. Nothing can be more frustrating than trying to fit a 10-15 page story into an ordinary commercial size envelope. Remember that s.a.e. means STAMPED addressed envelope. Acknowledgement cards should be stamped too, and when using self-seal envelopes, do tuck the flap in so that it does not seal itself all too firmly long before it's needed.

If you move house before your entry is returned, make arrangements for your post to be forwarded to your new address: competition organisers cannot search through thousands of envelopes to change the address on yours, nor can they search through thousands of entries in order to make a correction to your manuscript! Finally, do try to post your entry in good time. If you leave it to the last minute, you will panic and do something silly, such as forget to sign your cheque, or leave it out altogether. Believe it or not, once or twice I have received a cheque without an entry, and sometimes received an entry without anything at all, not even an entry form.

You may think that some of this advice is too obviously basic, but all these things do happen - not just occasionally, but over and over again. The over-riding piece of advice is still to read the rules and abide by them - it's astonishing how many people just throw money away by not doing so."

Quartos Open Competition: The *Quartos* Competition offers a critique tick-sheet for every entry provided a s.a.e. accompanies each one. Often we receive several entries, some for different categories and only one envelope so this can lead to manuscripts being mislaid. As Abi Hughes-Edwards still acts as judge for the Open Competition's poetry category, we asked her to voice a few more of her observations:

Abi Hughes-Edwards:
"It is very heartening to see so many poets caring sufficiently about their work to present it properly. Whilst I have less to complain about than in previous years, there are still a few examples of dreadful presentation and gross ignorance to more than compensate my inactive but sadistic pen.

I kid you not, after labouring the point in the wake of previous competitions, I received a booklet bejewelled with sequins and supposedly magic symbols! Several other computer-art be-daubed verses have also littered my study, along with a plethora of dolphins, beds, seagulls and other objects of great interest to any Jung analyst. I am not an art critic, I am not interested in these terrible illustrations (neither, I suspect are other editors/judges), so please desist from decorating your work with them.

Again there were people who ignored the 40 line criteria and submitted well in excess: 72 was the highest and I was suitably unpleasant. One last point on presentation: I realise that lots of people cannot afford computer systems or decent typewriters. However, I would prefer a good hand-written poem to one where the typewriter is missing two vowels and a 't'. Fascinating stuff, but I don't think the world's quite ready for it.

I choose what I like, since anyone who has to read the volume of poetry that competitions produce is entitled to be as despotic as they please. Having said that, I am satisfied that past winners have written poetry that would spark the dullish imagination. The poems are such that once read, they return again and again; wonderful words, lines, verses that intrude themselves on the every-day. I have been haunted by many such beautiful ghosts.

Contrary to popular belief, judges do not, on the evening before deadline, sit down with a box of wine, a blindfold and a pin. I read every poem three, sometimes four times. I speak them aloud to double-check the sense and flow, something I fear some of you do not before sending. After this I finally start the task of placing the winners, a period of much trauma and paper shifting. Grumbling souls may still feel it's unfair but at least they know how much effort I've put into being so!"

The Ian St James Award: This is the UK's largest prize for short stories which attracts a large number of entries every year by offering the widest scope for publication than all the other competitions put together. According to best selling author, Ian St James who created the competition in 1989 ... "the awards have

169

always offered a better way for writers to take a first step towards a literary career ... there are now even more opportunities for publication and access to leading literary agents and publishers."

The Awards Calendar:

Stage one - each manuscript received is read by at least one of the team of readers. This team consists of professional people involved in the worlds of publishing and writing. Their task is to review each story on its merit and appraise accordingly.

Stage two arrives with the submission of critiques for recommended stories to the office of The New Writers Club where a small group of readers will select the eighty stories that will make up the short-lists.

Stage three commences following this procedure when - voting separately and without consultation - the judges reduce the short-list to the twenty Award winners: ten in each of the two categories.

Stage four is the culmination of the year - the annual Awards function when the top story in both categories will be announced.

In addition to handsome cash prizes, the twenty winning stories are published in the annual collection, while the shortlisted stories in both categories (over 3,000 words and under 3,000 words) are published throughout the year in *Acclaim* Magazine and receive payment on publication. Merric Davidson, literary agent and administrator for the **New Writers' Club** which organises the Award, has the following advice for prospective entrants:

Merric Davidson:

"Over-writing is one of the most common problems that our readers come across in appraising short stories entered for the Awards. Good ideas can be submerged in over-explanation, flowery-prose and a large cast list. Impact goes out of the window and interest is lost. Keep it simple, keep it sharp, and beware too many viewpoints. Small is beautiful, but let the story be as short or as long as it needs to be. An 8,000 word story can be full of sub-plot and suspense, but so can one of 3,000. The all-important factor is not to stretch the idea."

As one of the Stage One readers for the Ian St James Awards, Christine Hall has shared some of the responsibility of selecting and short-listing the best stories from the huge number of entries.

Christine Hall:
"A considerable responsibility, because whatever I discarded was not re-read by anyone else. I read each entry at least twice looking for the four criteria which are particularly important for the Ian St James Awards: plot, dialogue, characterisation and pace. If a story excelled in three of these, I recommended it for the short-list. The most frequent weaknesses in otherwise promising stories were:
a) Slow beginnings.
b) Authors begin with lengthy introductions instead of action.
c) Too many explanations.
d) Don't explain characters (let them act) or situations (let them happen).
e) Flashbacks which are too frequent and/or too long. They slow down the pace.
f) Frequent and unnecessary switches of viewpoint. They keep your readers at a distance and prevent them from feeling with your characters. Unless the plot demands it, a short story is best told from one person's viewpoint.
g) Over-writing. e.g. a 3000 word when the plot would be suitable for a 800 word story. Many stories would benefit from trimming.
h) Little or no dialogue. Good dialogue characterises the protagonists, carries the plot forward, and makes explanations unnecessary.
i) Poor characterisation. By developing a c.v. for all the main characters before you start writing, you can give your story impact and credibility.
j) Typical beginner's twist endings: The central character commits suicide; the narrator turns out to be a cat; psychiatric doctor turns out to be a patient; murder by dropping electric appliance into bath; murderer manipulates brakes and uses car himself; hortensias change colour

171

where murder weapon is hidden; narrator wakes up and it was all a dream."

Merric Davidson:

"We all know that there is 'nothing new under the sun'. However, a competition reader is looking for a new and original slant, not necessarily a twist in the tail, although this can be satisfying. A 'new voice' can be much more rewarding. New writers should always be encouraged to search for their own voice. This doesn't come overnight and the search may take thousands of words.

Equally as important, never be satisfied with your story until you have carried out many hours of brutal revision. Often the first scenes that should go are the scenes that you were originally most pleased with!

There is no restriction on subject matter in the annual Ian St James Awards. Our readers are equipped to read in any genre, so look for some area that hasn't been overdone. That means some research reading could be required. For example, I can't recall reading a historical murder mystery in the seven years that I have been associated with these Awards!"

Acclaim Magazine provides one of the best 'writer's tools' for short story writers. Many would-be fiction writers insist on sticking to styles that are noticeably outdated and therefore totally unsuitable for publication in modern magazines. *Acclaim* gives some fine examples of contemporary fiction writing and in particular those gripping, visual first lines that makes the judge (or an editor) want to read on. Leo Llewellyn picked the following example from the 1994 short-list:

"They were lying on a double mattress under their double duvet, like corpses ..." (*The Kiss of Janus* - Chantal Porter)

"I disengage my handbag from the teabags in the bottom drawer of my desk, and cross the hall to the Ancient Monument which passes for a ladies toilet ..." (*Lioness* - Sarah Starkey)

"Mrs Spring was floating face down in the pool when her gardener found her. She hung there, half submerged, tangled in a length of filtration pipe ..." (*Butterfly Wings* - Peter Guttridge)

"I was seven years old when my mother died. Ancient aunts with thin, papery skins, smelling of eau de Cologne, took me in as a temporary measure. Just until my father came to claim me ..."
(*Bread & Butter* - Brigid Johnson)

"The Great Leon Stathakis, leader of the Athens Philharmonic Orchestra, had slid out of tune. Just perceptibly. Nobody mentioned it, of course ..." (*Discord* - Sue Camarados)

Each opening takes the reader right to the very heart of the story, cutting out the pages of 'scene setting' favoured by amateur writers. Here we have a story in miniature, so perfectly created that we must read on to discover who, what, why? This is exactly what an editor or competition judge wants to read - something that immediately elevates the manuscript high above the banal and mundane openings of the hundreds of other manuscripts waiting to be read. The importance of the opening lines can never be overstated, if you can produce a mind numbing opening similar to any of the above, you're on your way to writing marketable fiction.

As Leo Llewellyn commented in his article on the subject: "Having ploughed my way through the entries in a recent competition, it was surprising how many good writers fail to recognise the importance of the opening lines. Some really first class stories failed to reach my short-list purely on the grounds of a long-winded and unnecessary preamble to set the scene. All writing - whether it be a poem, article, full-length non-fiction, short story, novel or biography - needs opening impact. It is what makes your work stand out from the meandering outpourings of others. And, as so many other competition judges before me have observed, most short stories submitted would be drastically improved if the first one and a half pages were deleted! So, whether writing romance or horror the message is the same. Dispense with the urge to include a complete DNA of your character for starters ... keep your descriptions to a minimum ... avoid pages of boring dialogue. Keep it short, sharp and succinct; concentrate on drama and impact for maximum effect."

Swanage Poetry Competition: Having organised the Swanage Midsummer Festival competition since its inauguration seven years ago, with hundreds of poems passing through their hands annually, Lewis Hosegood, felt a summary of the judges' reactions might be helpful, together with some advice on what to offer, and perhaps more specifically - what to avoid.

Lewis Hosegood:
"On the down-to-earth side the first piece of advice, obvious though it may seem, is to read the rules - carefully! You'd be surprised how many entrants don't. (Are poets particularly unworldly perhaps?) Some competitions insist on an entry form; others require titles, names and addresses in a separate envelope. Anyway, don't type anything but the title on the entry itself - the organisers have to block it out, which wastes time.

Pay particular attention to any stipulation like submitting only unpublished work, or not entering it elsewhere. It's embarrassing if it wins two concurrent competitions and the organisers usually check. Don't forget the s.a.e. if you want your poems back - but some competitions won't return them anyway. A small s.a.e. marked 'results' should ensure you're notified of these. And do make sure you signed and dated the cheque properly - that's another common time and postage waster.

The actual presentation is important and although you won't be judged on neatness alone, it helps. Remember they'll probably have a great many entries to read and a judge's good nature may be adversely taxed by very faint type on flimsy, dog-eared paper which has clearly come back from other attempts. White paper is preferable to green re-cycled, even if you feel impelled to make a social statement. Do keep to A4 size as a standard format stacks easily together for judging.

Now the poem itself. The first thing to decide is what form it's to take. In the open competition there's room for all kinds - formal, with or without rhyme, free verse ... each has its advantages and pitfalls. A formal shape like a sonnet or triolet is pleasing, but don't let it become a jelly mould in which natural thought and language are constricted. If you choose formal meter (i.e. iambic) don't let it become a rigid dog-trot throughout. Occasional variation gives life - you will find examples of hop-skip rhythm changes in all the great poets, from Shakespeare to Larkin.

To rhyme or otherwise is usually a matter of choice. It is certainly back in favour today. The great thing is not to let it dictate the flow of expression. Too often one feels that the poet has thought of the rhyme first and then forced the words and sentiment to fit. This especially in conjunction with a too regular beat, produces a jingle - which is definitely not poetry. Rhyme seems to lend itself best to humorous verse. But note that very few humorous poems ever win open competitions. Many people don't realise the exciting possibilities of using rhyme alternatives - deliberate half-rhymes, internal rhymes (instead of always at the end of lines), assonance (i.e. vowel similarity and sprung rhymes (in irregular places). Don't be afraid to experiment.

Another thing which is not poetry, is prose chopped up into lines or verses to look like poetry. Competition organisers see plenty of this type. One test is to read it aloud - does it sound like poetry? Another is to write it out as a paragraph, as in prose. Would a casual reader be able to spot the difference? (Judges of my acquaintance try both these tests.) In free verse there should be an inevitability to the line lengths which depends upon the cadency of speech rhythms.

A mark of true poetry is the intensity, vividness and freshness of its language. Avoid cliches such as 'emerald grass' and 'azure skies' - see the grass and sky for yourself and paint your own picture. Avoid archaisms like 'twixt, 'twere, 'neath', 'o'er the heavens'. Remember: prefer metaphor to simile - it's stronger. Verbs are often stronger than adjectives - 'beaded bubbles winking at the brim'. The unusual, off-beat word can illuminate a line but beware of being too clever; it can have a reverse effect if you miss. Poetry can, and should, contain an element of mystery - but if it becomes totally obscure then something is wrong. You've squandered your trump-card - sympathetic communication.

Finally, I think my chief piece of advice to all entrants would be: Read widely. From all too many pieces received, one would think that 'modern' poetry was confined to Rupert Brook, John Betjemen and Kipling. It's also not a bad idea to try and read some of the adjudicator's own poetry. Although you can't 'analyse the market' quite as you would for a magazine, it might give you an idea of the judge's taste. But in the end, go by your own heart. Sincerity is all. Without it no true poem was ever written. Just try to be different."

To Return, Or Not To Return:

Not all complaints about competitions come from the organisers. Over the years, John Copley has been quite scathing on the subject of competition organisers and expressed the opinion that some were 'a blatant con'.

"When you think of it, it's the easiest thing in the world to rake in the entry fees and then call it a day. Certainly no need to judge, or even read the stories. And why bother to return them? ... Many do seem to need a remarkable amount of time to get the job done. Agreed, sifting through the entries, and getting the judges assembled for a final decision may take some time but does it really require months on end? Most people I know could stick a hundred stories into ready-addressed envelopes, lick 'em, stick 'em and bung them all in the post in about half an hour flat ... The writers have done 99% of the work, the returning bit should be easy."

Past organiser of an extremely popular national competition, Margaret Finch, deeply resented the insinuations and was quick to point out that her competition was organised by a small writers' group with no previous experience to draw on, and no funding apart from the entry fees which were used for prizes, judges' fees and other expenses.

She continued: "It may only take minutes to read a manuscript, but assessing and comparing them is altogether different, often requiring several scrutinies of each one. The last week before the closing date is chaotic and it is the last-minuters who actually hold up the proceedings. Each entry is read by six experienced writers, briefed by the judge, who only meet up once a week. The final selection for the judge's decision can only be made when the first reading has been completed. There is no way we can hustle that operation and still be fair to the contestants."

There is a considerable amount of criticism over competition organisers not returning manuscripts after judging, even though the majority state quite clearly in the rules that entries will not be returned. A number of Bridport competitors expressed their concern over what happened to their manuscripts once the competition was over and whether their ideas could be stolen by less scrupulous writers.

Peggy Chapman-Andrews used to keep them for a year before destroying them, but as space is limited, Bridport borrow a shredder to solve the problem of disposal so there is no question of ideas falling into other hands. *Quartos* used to destroy them via the kitchen Rayburn and as the numbers increased via garden incinerator and compost heap - now we give a critique for each entry (providing a s.a.e. is enclosed) and the manuscripts are returned to the author.

The non-return of manuscripts arouses passion; Margaret Finch, even had a complaint on the subject registered during Sunday lunch, by a chap who went to great lengths to explain that he did not allow fellow writers to enter competitions which did not return manuscripts. There is a good reason for this, as Margaret pointed out.

Once the competition is over and each entry has been read (sometimes several times over by the selectors), the pages have all manner of numbers, initials, question marks and notes scrawled in the margins; holes punched in them for ring binders and are consequently totally useless for re-submission elsewhere. However, the best of her stories concerned the entrant so lacking in imagination that she asked: "How could the organisers make a list of the prize-winners, when the rules stated that no names must appear on the manuscripts?"

One last word of warning about entering work for competition comes from Susan Alison. Having entered her poetry for Competition A, she waited until after the results had been announced (her name was not amongst the winners) before re-submitting the same unpublished poem to Competition B. In the meantime, she received a letter from Competition A informing her that although her poem was not amongst the winners, they were going to include it in their anthology.

This, of course, put our reader in an embarrassing predicament. By being included in the anthology, her submission for Competition B was null and void since the rules clearly stated that all entries were to be unpublished and not under offer elsewhere. Her problems were as follows:

1) Did she write to Competition B and withdraw her entry before the results were announced?
2) Write to Competition A and inform them that she did not want her poem included in the anthology?
3) Should she keep quiet since Competition A's anthology would not be due until well after Competition B's results were announced?

There was no cut and dried solution. Since Competition A was slow off the mark in informing her that the entry was to be included in their anthology, it would serve them right if it were withdrawn having won a place in Competition B. However, since the poem was still under offer, as it were, to Competition A, the organisers of Competition B would be well within their rights to disqualify the entry, even if it had not yet appeared in print. Since our reader was anxious to see her work published, and Competition A was offering this, she decided to keep quiet unless her poem was selected amongst the winners in Competition B. "I think I'll cross that hurdle when I come to it," she said.

As you can see, entering material for a competition does have its drawbacks - you can have short stories or poems tied up for months on end and if you have the opportunity to submit elsewhere you could risk disqualification if your winning entry is found to have been published in another magazine or anthology. Like magazine editors, competition organisers are not always fair but they do provide a large number of outlets for work which would normally be difficult to place. The choice of whether you support the competitions is yours, and yours alone.

Recommended Reading:

Acclaim Magazine is a bi-monthly publication featuring all the short-listed entries from the Ian St James Award. Not only does it provide good examples of cross genre contemporary fiction, it also lists current writing competitions and fiction outlets as well as articles on short story writing. It is a good general guide to writing for competition while being crammed with first class fiction. A sample back issue can be obtained by sending a 43p stamp (see contact addresses) ISSN: 0967-0289

Chapter 9 The Small Press

As indicated in previous chapters, the widest marketplace for freelance writers comes under the banner of what is generally referred to as 'the small press'. This outlet consists of hundreds of privately owned publications catering for every type of interest from kite-making to the occult, with every style of literary taste catered for in poetry and fiction. The Small or Independent Press can generally be described as falling into two categories:

a) Small privately operated and specialist publishing houses that produce between one to ten books per year as per those listed *The Writer's Handbook*. Unless your full-length manuscript or poetry collection falls within an extremely tight specification, don't waste your time approaching them;

or

b) Privately produced magazines that do not appear on the shelves of the local newsagents because of the low print runs and are usually only obtainable on subscription direct from the publisher. These cover the majority of literary magazines {*Staple, Metropolitan and The Third Alternative, Tees Valley WRITER*}; hobbyist/special interest publications produced by groups and organisations in the form of a regular magazine or newsletter {*Phoenix* (esoteria), *The British Archer* (sport), *Quartos* (creative writing), *Picture Postcard Monthly* (collecting), *Bird Watch Monthly* (nature), *Zene* (small press guide)}; journals of societies or professions {The Gothic Society's quarterly *Udolpho, Journal of Alternative & Complementary Medicine* and *Money Marketing*}. Although the publications are aimed at a specific group of people, most will accept freelance contributions but you are still advised to study a current copy of the magazine before submitting.

What are the problems?

The main difficulty for new writers is knowing where to locate details of Small Press publications. *1000 Markets for Freelance Writers* lists a number of low circulation, specialist interest publications; *The Writer's Handbook* updates its small press poetry magazine listing yearly, while writers' publications such as *PAPLI* (Association of Little Presses), *Writer's Guide*, *Zene* and *Small Presses & Little Magazines of the UK & Ireland* list dozens of magazines willing to accept poetry and fiction from freelance writers.

Although some receive regular grants from the Arts Council or Regional Arts Boards, many more rely solely on subscriptions and find it difficult to survive in the cooling economic climate. Our research shows that when recession bites, one of the first cut-backs appear to be magazine subscriptions. Since there are more people wanting to contribute to the magazines than there are paying subscribers, it doesn't take a mathematical genius to work out that the finances of such publications are precarious indeed.

Beginners, however, and even the more experienced writers, need to put the Small Press into perspective and understand how the system works, because very few people appreciate that most small press magazines are operated on a part-time, shoe-string budget. Potential contributors rarely consider the editor(s) may have a full time job and a tight production schedule of a reputable magazine often interferes with the editor's own writing activities. Perhaps one of the most common editorial complaints is of the many writers who refuse to take the Small Press seriously.

Nevertheless the Small Presses offer a wide ranging collection of styles and quality, ranging from the expensive glossy to the poorly photocopied; from brilliant snatches of contemporary literature to the down-right banal. Everyone's style and taste is catered for and the new-comer may find it easier to experiment with a change of approach among the Small Press publications. Small presses can also provide much needed shot-in-the-arm

181

acceptance when enthusiasm and confidence is at its lowest ebb because you can't break into the big-time.

I recently overheard, at a Small Press fair, the rather naive criticism that it was wrong that small press magazines were edited by people who 'had no money and insufficient time to produce a really professional magazine'. An observation which totally ignores the fact that if this band of dedicated people didn't edit such 'amateur' publications, hundreds of magazines wouldn't exist at all and the majority of beginners would be hard pressed to find suitable outlets for their work. Unfortunately for the Small Press editor, he receives more brick-bats than bouquets for his efforts.

Yes, of course, many of them are elitist and cater for a small minority of favoured contributors/readers; and yearly there are dozens which start with a flurry of publicity and then decamp with the subscription money. There will always be editors who sit on manuscripts for months on end and refuse to answer query letters - this happens just as frequently when submitting to the nationals - but do bear in mind the editor of a Small Press magazine may have to sort through piles of totally unsuitable manuscripts when he has just completed eight hours in a day-job. Spiteful comments from a frustrated writer aren't going to improve his humour or make her any the more receptive to the manuscript on offer.

Also remember the small press editor is autonomous. He has been running his publication for five, ten, twenty years and built up a strong nucleus of subscribers who like his particular brand of editorship. He rarely has to worry about keeping advertisers happy and providing the magazine appears on a regular basis, he sees little reason to change his style to suit anyone else. Those who persist in penning insults should also realise that the small press world is an extremely incestuous one, and most editors have a 'black list' of these literary abusers.

Who are the Small Presses?

Quartos began life in 1987 as a 12-page competition newsletter for writers and over the years developed into the 32-page creative writers' publication it is today. It started with a policy that aimed to

182

fill a gap in the marketplace at the time, and has never wanted to be anything else other than an exchange of information and creative ideas. Its success has been largely due to the fact that it is accessible and user-friendly - its subscribers have always been able to contact the Editor's desk by letter or telephone if a problem needs immediate attention. It also provides feedback on subscribers' work in the form of a critique which has enabled writers to re-examine their work before submitting elsewhere - with a very high success rate.

For the purpose of finding our way around the independent presses, I have used other Small/Independent Press publications which also appear to have found the right formula. Each one has built up a reputation of a high literary standard and represents different aspects of a Small Press editor's recipe for success.

Staple Magazine under the editorship of Don Measham and Bob Windsor has been in publication for over 10 years and is recognised as being one of the finest literary magazines in the UK, publishing both poetry and fiction.

Bob Windsor:

"Neither of us had any intention of starting a magazine but having made £15.00 profit following a writers' day, we decided to spend the surplus on postage stamps soliciting contributions from previous participants, with a view to publication in some form. Some 200 poems were received and although the original magazine was intended as a 'one-off ', publication, it continued with the encouragement of East Midlands Arts."

Don Measham:

"Success is relative - not a word we'd use. Our present position depends on the fact that we are not a clique, never publish on reputation alone, are absolutely open to all-comers, always need work (because we seldom or never carry writing over from one issue to the next), do enter into a dialogue with writers when we believe that it would be productive."

The Tees Valley WRITER, although its name suggests a localised nature, does in fact accept article, poems and fiction from much further afield. Started in 1990, it was part of the 'literary renaissance' on Teeside and as the Editor, Derek Gregory pointed out, they wanted to provide a voice and platform for local writers and play a part in identifying Teeside culturally. Publication is twice a year and a group of four to five on the Management Board make decisions on publication.

Derek Gregory:
"The decision to turn the magazine into a national publication with a national competition was largely on grounds of economic viability. In other words the magazine would have remained quite small with a small circulation and a less than professional appearance if we had remained purely local. It is a point of honour and pride, however, that the magazine preserves many features and points of contact with the region where it was born.

We wanted to produce a good, professional product at a reasonable price; to offer something different, and which does not abase itself entirely to the whims and fantasies of its readers. We abandoned the idea of starting small and gradually working our way up the ladder; we hadn't the patience for that."

A relative newcomer, *Metropolitan*, has developed a formidable reputation in a very short time and subtitles itself as a magazine of 'new urban fiction'. Founded by the current publishers, Elizabeth Baines, Ailsa Cox and John Ashbrook in 1992, the first issue was published in Autumn 1993.

Elizabeth Baines:
"The founding of the magazine was fuelled by the experience of all three of us as short-story writers. Over the previous ten years the number of magazine outlets for short stories had seriously diminished, and the traditional fostering ground for challenging literary fiction and new writers seemed to be in the process of disappearing. We wanted to redress the balance, to provide a new

184

outlet, and to create a platform for the kind of writing which we perceived as threatened by the commercial trends taking over publishing."

Ailsa Cox:

"In addition, in order not to fall into the same trap, we thought carefully about why so many literary magazines had disappeared: we realised that one problem was that grants were drying up everywhere. Our solution was to make some concessions to 'commercialism': we would have to make sure the magazine sold, and in order to do so we would have to make the design and format competitively professional.

There was also very much a literary-political dimension to this aspect of the project. As contributors to small magazines ourselves, we felt that on occasion our work had been little more than printed (rather than published. We felt that a true service to writers and literature would be to get new work out and around, bought in shops and read by more people than those committed ones who subscribe to literary magazines."

John Ashbrook:

"Right from the start we worked on establishing good design and wide spread, efficient bookshop distribution as well as literary quality. We quickly discovered that it was not possible to make shop sales profitable in straight financial terms, but our successful shop distribution creates a high profile for the magazine, which has considerable knock-on benefits, gaining us a reputation which has in turn secured us funding.

Since money is short, we do all this work ourselves (un-paid). Initially, an volunteer went 'repping' bookshops around the country; Elizabeth now personally handles a nationwide bookshop distribution (making the phone calls, typing up the invoices) as well as typesetting the magazine. Another volunteer, Ben White, does the design work while yet another helps out with subscription mail-outs. The three publishers conduct all of the publicity from designing leaflets to licking stamps."

Andy Cox is Editor of both *The Third Alternative* which caters for readers of stories and poetry in the horror, science fiction/fantasy genre and *Zene*, potentially the best guide to the independent presses in the UK and overseas.

Andy Cox:
"I'm a firm believer in gearing things with regard to the long term. So until we actually get something going that looks like it might work, I think we have to keep trying to actually raise the profile of the small press. Do some people think 'small = not worth bothering with'? We have to convince potential readers that it *is* worth bothering with. This is one of the reasons that I decided to print *The Third Alternative* and *Zene* on good quality glossy paper: in the long run, more people might realise that these publications are serious ventures with content and ambition."

The quality of a small press magazine, however, cannot guarantee its survival. Every editor has experienced more than a fair share of criticism via rude and insulting letters that writers would never dream of sending to a national magazine. Small press editors regularly receive letters from once-only readers who pounce on one sentence, twist it out of context and then proceed to write a three page epistle on why they considered a particular point of view to be rubbish/sexist/obscene, etc.

There is always the poem that offends because a reader decides its meaning is too obscure or risque. And very often a piece of modern fiction will bring an outburst because another reader doesn't consider it to be a 'proper story', i.e. no clearly defined beginning, middle and end. If the complainant spent as much time perfecting his work for publication, it might be better used than concocting banal letters to long suffering editors.

Letters To The Editor:
Apart from some not liking the feedback on critiques, the most frequent complaint about *Quartos* is levelled at the 'typos' appearing in the text. Since all manuscripts are electronically

186

scanned into a computer before being spell-checked, it often produces 'typos' such as 'that' instead of 'than' - 'as' instead of 'at' and the most popular deliberate mistake 'the judges' *derision* will be final' instead of 'the judges' decision with be final'. Experience has shown that the fact that one person is editor, typist, mail-sorter, fiction editor and tea-boy counts for nothing and despite painstaking explanations, there are always those who enjoy writing to complain - especially if you don't happen to choose their story for publication!

Andy Cox:

"Lately I've become concerned that the small press is seen as existing solely for writers. It gives too many false impressions: that the writing is somehow inferior because the writers can't get published in 'proper' journals, that it's just made up of sub-literate 'fanzines' run by sad people. Sure, magazines like *Zene* and *Quartos* are for writers (mostly), but I don't put together *The Third Alternative* for writers, I put it together for readers. I want it regarded on a level footing with so-called 'professional' literary magazines (and there aren't exactly many of those, are there?)"

Don Measham:

"People 'complain' by ceasing to subscribe. Those who stick with us like *Staple's* middle-of-the-roadness. Stylistically, that is - we're not afraid of controversy. The most valid complaint is that themes and treatment are sometimes too trivial/banal but 'Bathing Your Grandad' poems are typical of much of the general poetry scene today. Our answer is to think carefully before using such work, while reminding ourselves that in our book, it's worse to go to the other extreme: we don't readily respond to the impenetrable and pretentious. We do consciously from time to time, use work which we know will divide our readership but we don't go in for weird sex and violence - unless it's essential to a very good piece of writing! We have occasionally ruled out good writing on grounds that it might deprave or corrupt - e.g. work along the lines of paedophilia or crude racism."

Derek Gregory:

"Very few *TVW* readers/writers complain about the magazine, and if they do we always publish their letters. In the first place most writers want praise not criticism (which is very hard for a beginner to take) - so on that score it is strange that we get so few complaints. I imagine the readers who might have complained have voted with their cancellations! The second strange thing is that the complainant's letters merely reveal the pompous, self-regarding nature of the writer's attitude. We are not in the business of insulting readers - neither do we wish to lie to them for the sake of placation. The day when we start to cheat our readers will be the day we pack it in."

Elizabeth Baines:

"Actually, we've had hardly any complaints, but I can remember every single one we've had! Three bookshops stopped stocking us because their customers had commented that the magazine was too expensive for what it was. A complaint from Ireland that we charged one blanket fee for overseas subscriptions was fair comment and we changed the rates accordingly. One reader suggested we would be better in book format since the magazine tends to get chucked along with the *Radio Times*, etc; disposability didn't worry us over-much since we're in the business of creating literature in the making. *Metropolitan* isn't meant to be a collector's item but an agent of literary change. Finally, one rejected writer made a veiled but pained complaint that we didn't give him enough feedback when returning his manuscripts."

Where Does The Money Come From?

Apart from a small promotional grant from the Arts Council some years ago, *Quartos* has never been reliant on funding but is this true of the other magazines?

Derek Gregory:

"The *Tees Valley WRITER* is reliant on the Regional Arts Council for nearly half its funding."

Elizabeth Baines:
"Initially we received one-off grants from the North West Arts Board and Manchester City Council to conduct a feasibility study: at present we have ongoing funding from the North West Arts Board. We received a development grant from the Arts Council, and have just received a one-off sum from the Foundation for Sports & the Arts. This funding allows us to break even."

Don Measham:
"Yes, we received Arts Council funding because that's the direction in which *Staple* has developed - i.e local-national-international - but it no longer has any predetermined local/regional focus."

Andy Cox:
"Neither *The Third Alternative* or *Zene* are funded by the Arts Boards or anyone - we're independent and proud of it. The magazines are funded the same way as any other small press: sales and subscriptions. As the local Literature Officer has changed I might talk to them again, but I will not sacrifice my editorial integrity for their money (it seemed like that would happen when I approached them before)."

If a large majority of small press publications are subsidised or funded by the Arts Council or Regional Arts Boards, how would the withdrawal of funding affect publication?

Derek Gregory:
"If funding were withdrawn, or even substantially diminished, the magazine would cease to exist. Even the Royal Shakespeare Company requires massive funding. There is no case for supposing that any art can exist commercially in any significantly widespread sense; those who believe it can are guilty of self-deception. We have made this quite plain to our sponsors - as a Board we are prepared to work for nothing, but we are not prepared privately to finance the 'losses' on our publication."

Elizabeth Baines:

"We'd have to stop. We're already subsiding the magazine personally with our unpaid time, and inevitably, our own pockets, and we would not have the personal financial resources to make up the deficit. Our bookshop distribution is phenomenally successful for a small magazine but bookshop sales are not profitable. A greater cover price would make us unsaleable (some bookshops have already complained that it is too high for a magazine!), but at the present price we most often make a loss on shop sales: the book-shop takes 33-50% and the sum left after we've deducted the cost of postage, packing and 'phone calls does not cover the cost of print-ing each copy. Another problem with bookshops is that they can take up to two years to pay the money they owe on an issue, and grants help with the cash flow."

Bob Windsor:

"In the short-term we could survive without funding but only with even more unpaid effort by the Editors and we would have to become even more obviously a fund-raising operation. The *Staple* Open Poetry Competition would, for instance, have to become an annual event to bring in extra finances, and on present figures, with some cost-cutting, we would probably survive. That presupposes that (a) producing a *Staple* competition annually (at present biennially) wouldn't affect subscriptions to the magazine - since more competitions would not be welcomed by some subscribers; (b) that the bubble hasn't burst with regard to poetry competi-tions. We, too, have suffered from the National Lottery! Finally, (c) that the Editors would be willing to take on more and more the role of routine chore-mongers: not sure that we would want to."

Lowering the Standards?

A common criticism of many small press editors is that they will accept any old rubbish from subscribers, just to fill up the pages. The publications contributing to *From An Editor's Desk* have a reputation for quality content, so what sort of material gives them the greatest pleasure to receive?

Derek Gregory:
"Good imaginative material which shows that there is a non-lazy person out there with ambition to succeed and make life more interesting for all of us. Someone who wants to add something to the literary cuisine - not someone who chucks us just another fake pork pie!"

Don Measham:
"(i) To be the first to publish something by someone who looks to be a true writer; (ii) to be the first to publish something by someone who may not develop further as a writer, but because of his/her life experience has at least one uniquely fascinating story to tell or viewpoint to convey - it's as likely to be someone young or they may well be in the 50-80+ age range."

Elizabeth Baines:
"Well, clearly, the kind of story we instantly take to, can't put down and immediately feel impelled to publish - in other words, quality fiction that fits our ethos but is distinctive and original in itself."

Andy Cox:
"What type of material gives me pleasure to receive? Subscription cheques! Apart from that, I like to receive good stories for *TTA*: stuff that surprises me, that doesn't contain cliches. For *Zene*, it would be a refreshing angle on a subject relevant to writers, readers, editors and publishers: something intelligent, humorous or, best of all, controversial. I also take great joy in receiving sets of guidelines from publicatio␣ ␣ ␣ previously listed in *Zene*, and especially from publicatioi ␣␣␣ starting out. I relish their enthusiasm."

When I asked the Editors to give their most common complaints *against* potential contributors, however, they were all far more expansive and their comments bring us back to that vital lesson from Chapter 3 - the importance of market research.

191

Derek Gregory:

"Cliche! cliche! cliche! All right - a bit more specific. Writers who send material which is a clone of what editors of some popular magazines in the 30's used to accept from their golfing pals. So we are back to cliche! We also welcome new contributors because there are so many good writers waiting for publication that I think we should spread our favours around if possible. In fact, if we receive two pieces of equal merit we would be inclined to choose the contributor who hasn't appeared in the magazine before. Unfortunately having accepted one piece of their work, they frequently deluge us with the contents of their bottom drawer."

Elizabeth Baines:

"Most definitely the kind of material and accompanying letter which makes it quite clear that the sender has never set eyes on the magazine. If we can't make sales and build up subscriptions we will not keep going, but most writers seem quite unprepared to support the magazine which is in turn the life-blood for new writing and writers. Some potential contributors make a point of informing us, unprompted, that they can't afford to buy the magazine, but when a year's subscription to *Metropolitan* is only the price of three pints of beer, one can't help wondering if the statement reveals more about their priorities than their finances. I realise that many writers feel that as a potential contributor their role is different from that of readers and purchasers (that they're the suppliers not the receivers) but the sad fact is that the general public still needs to be persuaded of the importance of literary magazine fiction."

Alisa Cox:

"In addition, when material is totally off the mark there is a waste of our time. We are writers ourselves, giving up our time voluntarily to produce and run the magazine. We make a point of looking carefully at everything we receive but can ill afford the hours we have to spend sifting through the initial pages of wildly unsuitable material, packing it back in envelopes and sending explanatory notes.

Part of the same syndrome: manuscripts which arrive with indications of the assumption that we are some kind of script-processing service or writer's surgery. These are often without an accompanying letter at all (these are usually in the wildly unsuitable category and indicate lack of familiarity with the magazine), or with the request (sometimes demand!) for a critique should we decide not to publish the story. We have even had demands for lists of short-story outlets world-wide, along with details of their requirements!"

Bob Windsor:
"Those who send work without the least idea of the kind of thing we're likely to take; not that there's a formula, but it should be quite clear to anyone who's looked at the magazine that we're unlikely to take bland doggerel or genre fiction. Simultaneous submission - the practice seems on the decrease, mercifully. The lack of s.a.e.'s or International Reply Coupons. Silly sized return envelopes - huge or tiny. Vast quantities of work at one go; second and third submissions of similar work immediately after a rejection; embarrassingly conceited accompanying letters and c.v's and 'shrinking violets'. The other extreme - one minimalistic poem (a haiku maybe), or a one-paragraph story with no accompanying letter."

Elizabeth Baines:
"I suppose many writers feel that if a magazine is financed out of public funds then it should provide them with an inclusive service, but the public funds are meant to cover only the production costs of the magazine. To be brutally frank, our brief really does go no further than providing a platform to encourage the production of good literature, then picking out the good fiction that is sent in and launching it properly on the world - a full-time job in itself. As it happens, because of our intense personal interest in writing and desire to encourage the development of good writing and writers, we do comment when we can or feel it's appropriate, but we simply don't have the time to provide detailed commentaries for every manuscript.

To some extent, I guess, we are victims of our own professionalism - people don't imagine that we are writers too, juggling the running of *Metropolitan* with our own writing and the jobs we need to keep in order to live and support our families. The expectations that writers have of us, along with the lack of financial support the magazine gets from them on the whole, really is enough, at the worst moments, to make us feel like giving up."

Alisa Cox:

"Finally - and this probably sounds terrible - we can't stand return envelopes which are recycled and require us to get out the sellotape and tape them down: all very commendable environmentally, but try doing it when you've got a batch of 50 manuscripts to send back once a fortnight, on top of all the other mail involved in running a magazine - it can triple the time it takes to deal with packing a manuscript! For the same reason, we don't like those plastic envelopes that you have to fiddle about with and squeeze the manuscripts in and out. Anything which makes a manuscript hard to read or handle - faint ribbon, single spacing, handwriting - is going to jeopardize its chances."

Derek Gregory:

"On another theme, one of our pet peeves is the person who argues about why we were 'wrong' in rejecting their manuscript, as if we are public servants with duties applying set criteria. Using public money we do have certain responsibilities but, theoretically, we do not have to give reasons for our actions in this respect. Practically, if anyone wants to start their own magazines and start exercising their own judgements they are welcome to try. It is (all too) easy, just a few forms to fill in - and a mountain of work."

Andy Cox:

"My most common complaint against potential contributors is that often they haven't got a clue about what you publish. They haven't even bothered to find out the editor's name, and send you what is obviously a form letter, which is worse than no covering letter at all. That's so damned impolite. This sort of thing grates even more when you're knocking yourself out putting together something like *Zene*, one of whose aims is to help people avoid things like that. And too many people don't know that they should enclose a s.a.e. with their submissions/enquiries. There are a lot of wonderful potential contributors out there, of course. Many previous 'potential' contributors are now regular authors, here and elsewhere, and have become firm friends besides."

Payment:

Keeping a Small Press magazine afloat (even with Arts Council funding) is not an easy task. The majority of editors work on their publication for love rather than gain but the most common reason deterring writers from submitting material to the Small Presses, is the fact that very few make even a token payment for the material accepted for publication. For a magazine starting out with little or no funding, the prospect of paying contributors can be daunting but when you consider that the majority of Small Press magazines have been running for years without paying a penny for submissions, writers can be forgiven for thinking that this method of working is rather unfair.

Derek Gregory:

"On acceptance we publish, pay for, and send a complimentary copy to all contributors. Some of our payment is in the form of prizes for short stories and poetry; non-prizewinners who are published receive a token fee per printed page. Our feeling is that writers should be paid wherever possible. We are, of course, non-profit making, but if we have any kind of surplus, the first call on this would be to increase the payment to our authors."

Don Measham:

"We make a nominal payment of £5 per item, with £10 for three pages or more plus a complimentary copy. Payment is useful and/ or justifiable if it makes a writer take professional care: provided that 'professional' means 'I'll cross that out' or 'I won't send that out, it isn't good enough' - Dubious if it means: 'They didn't like that, but this might earn a fiver'."

Elizabeth Baines:
"We do pay contributors as a point of strong policy, and we would like to be able to pay them more. As professional writers ourselves, we take it as given that writers should be paid a fair price for their work. Unfortunately, like all small magazines we simply don't have the money to pay them what they are really worth. This has to be balanced with the provision of a platform which new writing and writers would not otherwise have, and which can pave their way to mainstream publishing."

To give a broad, over all assessment of how writers, tutors and editors feel about the Small and Independent Presses in general, I asked the contributors to voice their honest opinions as to the importance of Small Press magazines from the writers' point of view.

Peter Finch - published poet and author:
"Numerically the small presses and the little magazines are the largest publishers of new poetry, both in terms of range and total sales. They operate in a variety of shapes and sizes everywhere from Cardiff to Caithness and Lewes to Llandudno. This country's best poetry magazines all began as classic 'littles' - nonetheless between them they will get to almost everyone who matters."

Andy Cox - small press editor:
"Invaluable for writers of fiction and poetry, I would've thought, but a lousy place to earn money as a true professional freelance. In that respect, it's a fine way to practice your article writing, interview technique, etc. and maybe collect a few impressive publishing credits."

Graham Stevenson - freelance journalist and author:
"If it wasn't for the Small Presses, I probably wouldn't be doing

what I'm doing now. My first acceptance for a filler article led to the editor of a 'small' business magazine commissioning me to produce a series of business handbooks. Unfortunately, he died before publication and I was left with the manuscripts on my hands. Fortunately, the exercise wasn't wasted because the work had taught me how to apply my concentration to larger projects and I eventually sold all the manuscripts in article form to another small press editor for a very tidy sum. This encouraged me to take my writing seriously, eventually to try the national publications and write my non-fiction books."

Derek Gregory - small press editor:
"It is often said that the commercial opportunities to sell, even simply to have published, one's short stories or poems, are limited. They are worse than that. The opportunities for the non-famous writer are practically non-existent. If it were not for the small presses it would be pointless to practice these crafts. This may not always have been so, but anyone in the publishing field today knows this truth. The small presses are vital to the practice of the literary arts in this country."

Janie Jackson - writing tutor:
"I'm afraid our comments regarding the small press won't be popular. The small press (if we are referring to writing publications such as *Quartos, Writers' Forum, Flair Newsletter, etc.,*), can be extremely helpful to beginners - maybe more so than the more glossy, commercial writing magazines. When it comes to the small press magazines which publish short stories, etc. we query their usefulness. Undoubtedly, it gives new writers a boost to see their work in print, but frequent successes with the small press may well give them an exaggerated idea of their own abilities. In consequence, they tend to become resentful of rejection from commercial markets, and to confine their efforts to small press publications.

The type of stories used by small press magazines are seldom the sort which commercial markets use. Similar remarks apply to stories which win prizes in competitions. A case in point - one of our subscribers received a glowing report from the Ian St. James Award, with the comment that he would have no problem in selling the story. Several submissions later, he asked us for help in finding a market. We replied that, though the story was competently written, there simply wasn't a market for it. We feel that the small press, too, uses the type of material which is *not commercially viable.*

I suppose the brief answer is - if seeing your work in print is all that matters to you, then go for the small press. If you want to be *commercially* successful, study and write for the commercial markets. For these reasons, we don't encourage our subscribers to write for small press magazines, with the exception of those writing magazines mentioned above."

Don Measham - small press editor:

"Very important as a means of publication for new talent. Its importance is much less obvious to us with regard to those writers who write competently and inoffensively to clock up hundreds of published credits in a great many small magazines. It's depressing to see the same names recurring. It's probably too easy now to get poetry published somewhere in some form. There should, however, be more opportunities for non-genre short fiction - *Staple's* efforts in this field are beginning to be recognised, we feel."

Christine Hall - freelance journalist and writing tutor:

"Small presses play an important role in the UK publishing scene, and I believe that their importance will grow further in the future. As the big book and magazine publishing houses are contracting and reducing their lists to no-risk, profit-guaranteed, wide-interest titles, there remain niches in the market for special interest publications.

As a magazine/newspaper editor, and now editorial consultant and agent, I have always taken writers with a track record in small press writing very seriously. Some people believe it is easy to write for the small presses who will publish just about anything, but this is not so. Good small press editors are just as selective as commercial ones, only their criteria may be different. Small fiction presses may place less importance on commercial interest and instead apply higher literary standards.

Small non-fiction presses usually aim at a clearly defined readership; contributions to these will require less mass-market appeal but more specialist knowledge. But the most important criterion applies to contributors to all publications, whether they are small or big presses: that of being able to write what a particular readership wants.

Having said this, I believe that it is easier for the talented new writer to break into the small press market than into the big commercial publishing world. Small editors are more likely to judge a contribution by its literary merit than by the fame of the author's name. When writing for small publishers, you don't have the competition from professional writers, who have to earn a living from their work and therefore rarely bother to write for small presses which cannot pay high fees."

Elizabeth Baines - small press editor:

"Clearly, we'd never have invested this amount of unpaid time, energy and creativity if we didn't think it was of the utmost importance!"

Recommended Reading:

ZENE is new but it's a good value guide to the independent press. A mini-glossy quarterly, A5 36-page magazine packed with reviews, articles and profiles of the various small press publications and publishers. This is an inexpensive introduction to the Small Press and the magazine builds up into a useful reference section.
ISSN: 1355-5154

Chapter 10   Self-Publishing Without Tears

 During The London International Book Fair a seminar offering 'An Insider's Guide To Getting Published' produced a shocked reaction when participants were told by a leading literary agent, "It is the lot of agents and publishers to tactfully stop people writing books." Followed by the fact that only 1.05% of all manuscripts submitted to British and American publishers ever get into print, it would appear that the agent might have indeed stifled the literary aspirations of all but the most determined.

Today's mainstream publishing needs to be put into perspective; and so does the alternative - self publication. Not to be confused with vanity or subsidised publishing; self-publication, if undertaken correctly, can prove to be a rewarding experience both personally and financially.

A self-published print run of 500 paperbacks costs in the region of between £6-800.00; vanity or subsidy publishing can cost more in the region of £5000 according to the complaints received over the years at *Quartos* magazine. The message is loud and clear: *Never* be tempted to produce a book using vanity publishers even though their advertisements in the national broad sheet newspaper may be tempting.

Even experienced writers can be caught out: In the autumn 1992, Gill Redman met a subsidy publisher through a talk given at her local writers' circle and after discussing a few amendments she was asked for a 'contribution of £600 towards production costs'. The book was scheduled for publication to coincide with the

London Book Fair the following spring but despite a stream of letters, galley-proofs and excuses from the publisher, the book was still not in print two years later. Although she received a complimentary copy of the first book in the series, there was no letter and no information concerning her own book which was the second title accepted.

Finally, in exasperation, Gill Redman sent recorded letters to both addresses listed for the publisher, stating that the right to publish would be withdrawn as from the 31st December 1994. Both letters were signed for; she even received a picture postcard apologising for the delay but since then she has had no further contact from the publisher and is £600 the poorer.

"If it stops others from being as naive as I was, it's worth any publicity you can give it. At least, I now have the papers sorted and am ready to contact a solicitor, though the Citizen's Advice Bureau warns me that action will cost me more money and I may win nothing in the end!" she wrote.

The beginner often believes that once his/her manuscript has been accepted by a reputable publishing house, all problems promptly cease. This is not always the case and horror stories abound about books that have been 'remaindered' or 'pulped' only two or three weeks after release because the sales figures do not come up to expectations. Remaindered books often go on sale at greatly reduced prices through high street cut-price shops, while pulped means exactly that. Either way, the author has little in his pocket to show for months or even years, of hard work.

Caught up in the back-lash of pulped or remained publications, the author's interests can also be tied up for the remaining period of their contract with the publisher, unless the small print states that the rights return to the author in the event of the book being removed from the publisher's listing.

The name of the game is ££££'s: if your book fails to be financially viable, it will be withdrawn immediately and even if you do manage to find an alternative imprint, you may experience difficulties in persuading the original publisher to release you from your contract.   One of the most important reasons for self-publication is that it gives you total control over how long your book remains in print.

Ask Yourself Why?

Trevor Lockwood of the Author-Publisher Network came up with this observation: "At the present moment, in Great Britain, about 250,000 people are writing a novel, short story or poem. Last year the country published just under 70,000 books. The majority of these were non-fictional works ranging from repair manuals to great legal tomes.

The writer of fiction has a better chance of finding a publisher than they do of winning the National Lottery, but they will find the writing process will be much more expensive, not just in creative blood loss but in pennies spent in the Post Office, with British Telecom and in stationery and computer shops. What rewards are likely to come from this effort? The question - what does the writer expect to achieve from publication of their work - suggests another question that must be asked by the writer. What do they want from writing?"

Obviously the answer to both questions is publication and financial reward. But if it is almost impossible to get your foot in the door of the mainstream publishing houses and many of the small press publishers restrict their listings to a chosen few, there *is* only one alternative - self-publication.

The next question you need to ask yourself is: what are you going to do with the finished product? While the fourth question should be: Why do you want your book in print?

The answer to all four questions is the lynch-pin on which the whole self-publishing exercise will hang, because if you don't understand *where you're going* from the very beginning, the enterprise could cost you a lot of money - with very little result other than the spare bedroom (or worse, a leaking garage!) stacked high with unsaleable books, an empty bank account and a badly dented ego.

Self-publishing allows you to control how much you spend, because as Nancy Smith points out in *Writing Your Life Story*, vanity publishers usually prove to be extremely expensive with you bearing all the production costs, regardless of anything suggested to the contrary.

A Personal Tale:

My own non-fiction manuscript for the *Malleus* had been doing the rounds of publishers and agents for two years and with rejections such as ...

"Many thanks for sending me this (MS) which I really enjoyed."
"It is an excellent work."
"I recognise its importance and value."
"I confidently expect to see it published one day."
"A very thorough, well written and readable treatment of the subject."
"Your work is interesting and unusual, and there should be a market for it."
"an excellent job ..."
"I read the manuscript with great interest."

... it seemed ridiculous to leave it gathering dust while publishers reduced their listings to a safe, bare minimum. It was obvious that I had a manuscript that had provoked more than a modicum of interest - even if they weren't buying!

The idiocy of the situation was compounded by insider information received from a well-known literary agent; that the publishing industry had reached the point where many were refusing to read any more new authors, and that some had specifically asked not to be sent anything other than 'established names' or obviously commercial non-fiction such as the Royal Family, showbiz biographies and health books.

Around the same time, having joined the Society of Authors and become a founder member of The Author-Publisher Network (although only in the early stages of its development, A-PN offered a potentially invaluable support group for anyone indulging in serious self-publishing), I was tempted to go it alone.

Added to this, an advance copy of *The Writer's Handbook* arrived, featuring an article by first-time novelist Adrian Hill - 'If You Can't Join Them, Beat Them' who had decided to go for self-publication.

There appeared to be a general pattern of thinking, even amongst previously published writers, that the future trend (except for the really big names) will be for lesser known writers to self-publish and market their own books. This idea seemed even more sensible when publishing gossip confirmed the awful truth that slow moving books can be 'pulped' within weeks of release. If the big, main-stream publishers were out, it appeared to be the only sensible solution.

The Best-Sellers:

So how do you decide whether you have a book that is worth the time, effort and expense of self-publication? Again we go back to the most important facet of the writer's craft: Market research! Non-fiction books of local interest, or specialist subjects have a ready-made market place which needs to be fully explored BEFORE you decide on anything else. There are all sorts of peculiarities surrounding book selling and it's wise to know in advance of any pitfalls that, had you taken a different tack initially, could have saved you time/money, etc.

In the case of my own book, I already had a contact who had given a considerable amount of help at the research stages of the *Malleus* - he also had a regular mail order outlet of some 40,000 addresses which he was willing to put at my disposal! If I produced my own advertising material for insertion, one of these order forms could be included in every mailing. An agreement was made for a 40% discount for all books sold through this method, which was in line with standard booksellers' discount (between 25-40%), and hopefully the quantity of sales would justify the price.

This was a ready-made market-place for esoteric non-fiction works, but almost all specialist subjects have their own magazine, society, organisation, etc., and the outlets offered by these methods of advertising should influence your decision whether to go ahead with your book. You must ensure that you will be able to reach the right target audience but don't take it for granted that affiliated groups or publications will be willing to support you - ask first and get their agreement in writing.

Local authors usually get a warm reception from booksellers and libraries but you'll need the finished product before you attempt to interest them. Local history has a ready-made marketplace providing you choose an approach, area or subject not already covered. As one of our contributors who had self-published an extremely successful local history book explained: "People like to read original material, especially if it relates to a familiar place or subject." While another, who self-published 1000 books on a local history in Wales, was sold out within weeks; she's just produced a second volume, complete with old photographs, for which local bookshops (including W. H. Smith) are clamouring.

Victor Brown, having had his children's novel rejected by "all the recognised publishers", decided to go in for self-publishing following *The Huntrodd's Eye* being accepted for serialisation on local radio. The story had been broadcast during the summer and repeated two years later. As a result, the author was "approached by a local school who had been searching in vain for the non-existent book. I supplied them with the manuscript which they copied and now, when the school goes to Whitby to study how a writer's work is influenced by location, they use my book and not Bram Stoker's *Dracula* as they had done previously."

Distribution has always been the bug-bear for self-publishers and it's something to which the Author-Publisher Network is paying special attention. In the meantime, however, knowing where you're going to sell the book is almost as important as writing it, so make sure you've done your homework. Distribution is not the only problem; self-publishing runs certain risks that are normally covered by publishers and you'll need to make doubly sure that you're not infringing anyone's copyright, or committing unintentional libel, which could result in the whole lot being scrapped, or worse still, costing you a considerable amount of money in legal costs. The Society of Authors provide guidelines covering libel and the new laws on copyright which can be obtained for £1 each if you are not a member.

Doing Your Homework:

Once you've made the tentative decision to go ahead with self-publishing, the next step is to find out how much it's going to cost. We discussed the possibilities with the printing firm who produces *Quartos Magazine*, to see if there was any way we could produce a paperback book and avoid dealing with another, untried printing company. This was not as simple as it sounded.

Whereas we use a commercial printer for the magazine, they are not set up for book production; this meant that certain stages of production would have to be contracted out and subsequently push the price up because they would have to pay outside firms to carry out the work. What we did have, however, was a valuable safety advisor.

Lesson One:
All printers can probably do the job but a specialist short-run book publisher will probably give a better price.

The second option was to produce the book ourselves, so we spent some time investigating the possibility of purchasing additional computer equipment and software to enable us to do this. The system was impressive and the end product was an attractive paperback; on the minus side, it would have cost us several thousand pounds to acquire the system and there were some anomalies over the projected life-span of the equipment. Although it would have been possible to produce a book at under £1 per copy, we weren't too happy with the binding (which could be solved by purchasing a more expensive binding machine), but we would still need to go to a printer to have the outside cover printed and the finished book trimmed.

Lesson Two:
Even though an idea looks impressive and the costs seem right, don't rush into any commitment until you've completed your homework, especially if this means purchasing additional equipment.

I decided to take the advice of The Author-Publisher Network and find a small-run publisher who could undertake the whole production at a reasonable price for a first book, thereby not getting bogged down in the intricacies of self-production - our printer agreed. We contacted several publishers who specialised in short-run book production and here the differences in attitude, capabilities and end result were monumental.

Having been warned by *our* printer that methods of binding varied considerably from a poorly glued volume that cracked the first time the book was opened, to a tough stitched hardback, we were determined to acquire samples before taking the discussions further - and this highlighted another problem. Most were *unwilling* to send a sample copy of previously published books to give an example of their work; others sent wads of paper samples but no indication of cost or quality of the finished product, even though we were, by this time, able to give the exact number of pages, number of print run, type of cover required, etc.

Lesson Three:
If you can't get straightforward, informative answers, don't bother to continue discussions. If there's a problem in production, you may not be able to get an answer then, either.

I went back to A-PN and finally settled on Antony Rowe Limited (Bumper's Farm, Chippenham, Wiltshire SN14 6QA) for a variety of reasons. Firstly, the staff listened, asked the right questions and promptly sent two estimates for different styles and samples of their work. Secondly, they had a sense of humour, and as book production takes a while, it was nice to know there was someone with whom you could establish a good rapport while the work was being carried out - (especially if you felt the need to indulge in a bit of hysteria). They are used to people who are producing a book for the first time and know how to answer the questions. Thirdly, they don't mind you changing your mind. We were originally going for a 250 book print run (200 pages) and was sorely tempted by their extremely high quality hardback, but finally decided on a 1000 book print run in paperback.

Lesson Four:
Always acquire samples of the publisher's previous work and don't be frightened to ask for comparable estimates. If the company won't supply sample books, don't deal with them because you will have no idea of what their finished product will look like.

The decision to increase the print run was influenced in the main by the fact that there was that large mail order outlet to be catered for, and because it would cost us the same price again if we wanted a further 250 copies (because the publisher doesn't keep the plates, setting up the re-run from scratch), we decided to take the gamble and go for an increased first printing. By writing on a specialist subject, you should have researched the ready-made market place in similar interest magazines and specialist bookshops, so check again just how much advance publicity you can get from review copies and reviews.

Lesson Five:
Have a firm idea of how you are going to sell the book. By registering the title through Whitaker's, your book will appear on the national register and a few orders will filter through, but on the whole you're going to be responsible for marketing your own book.

Before embarking on larger print runs, do make sure that you have somewhere to store them. 1000 books are heavy and take up a lot of room; and if they're going to lay around for a while, they will discolour badly while in storage. We've seen examples of this from mainstream publishers, so if you're unsure of how many people will want to read your book it is probably best to keep the numbers low.

Lesson Six:
Don't over estimate the number of books you think you can sell, especially if you are thinking of producing a novel. Be realistic.

Spend some time thinking about the presentation of the book and try to use the most eye-catching design for your cover. We commissioned a local illustrator to produce something original, rather than use obvious library pictures or straightforward text. You will be asked to provide the art work for the cover, so start paying some thought to the effect you want to achieve - this is definitely not a last minute thing to decide on. Have a look at the current titles in your local bookstore and see if they spark off any ideas for design.

Lesson Seven:
Attempt to produce the most attractive book you can afford. It needs to tempt the buyer (bookseller and reader) and compete with major publishing houses who spend fortunes on cover design.

and finally ...

Lesson Eight:
There is no cheap and easy way to publish your own books. There are right ways and wrong ways and the only person to blame if you get it wrong, is yourself!

There are various methods of preparing a manuscript for publishing and much of this depends on whether you are submitting it as hard-copy, i.e. a complete typed manuscript, or on disk in TEXT/ACSII format (see Chapter 1). Check with the publisher which form he requires, since there is usually a slight reduction in cost if the manuscript is readily available on disk. Remember - *all corrections are your responsibility* - there is no liability on the publisher's part to correct or point out any errors in the text. On the hard copy (which should also accompany the disk) any alterations should be made above the line, within the double-spacing; italics should be underlined and any words in bold should be underlined with a wavy line.

When submitting the manuscript, never, send the only copy, or you are asking for trouble. Include any preliminary pages that are required, including title, author, publisher's name (imprint), address, author's notes, dedication, contents page and index (if applicable), any end pages, together with all illustrations to be used and the ISBN - International Standard Book Number - in the form of a computerised bar code.

Send the cover illustration (with photographs if any are being used) between two sheets of cardboard and attach your 'blurb' which should appear on the back of the book to persuade the idle browser to buy. This short piece of text needs to outline the purpose of the book or the story, and give a good reason why someone should want to read it. Don't leave it until you are ready to send everything off to the printer - it is one of the most important things you will ever write!

I recently attended a writers' day on self-publishing and a small press publisher of many year's experience announced that she had only discovered she had problems with the printing when she took delivery of the whole load and found that the title and author's name had been left off the spine! A good printer should have noticed this and queried it but it shows that even highly experienced folk still can (and do) make mistakes.

Was it worth it?

As a bookseller, Victor Brown, reckoned to know something about marketing and "the fact that my book was set in one of the most popular tourist areas in the UK ought to give it maximum exposure." A year after his article appeared in *Quartos*, I asked Victor Brown about the sales of his novel and whether he would do it again: He repeated that if he felt he had the right manuscript, he would go ahead.

When Iris Bryce's canal boat series went out of print she was still receiving regular requests for the first book *Canals Are My Home* and although she approached the original publisher to discuss the possibility of a re-print, there had been a change in editorial policy and they were no longer interested in the subject. After a series of false starts and promises, the author decided to go ahead and self-publish the title, selling the books locally herself.

Iris Bryce:

"I receive one or two orders each week from various libraries in England, and of course there's the chance of earning PLR as well. In totting up the sales figures we found that we'd sold over 400 and managed to repay a third of our 'borrowed' savings within a few months."

Lewis Hosegood

"Why did I decide to enter the notoriously difficult field of self-publishing? I'm afraid the simple truth is that if I could have found a 'real' publisher for it I would gladly have done so. The manuscript however, was turned down by fourteen publishers and four agents, despite my track record (four novels with mainstream publishing houses). So I was left with two alternatives - either consign it to the rejects cupboard, or have a go at DIY. Since I continued to think the novel was one of the best things I'd ever done, I decided on the latter. I read works variously by Peter Finch, Charlie Bell, Shirley Read, Jacquelyn Luben and others on the subject and considered it worth trying. It's certainly proved difficult and I don't know that I would recommend it generally!"

There have, however, been some frightening revelations in the national press in recent months concerning mainstream publishing, which makes self-publishing seem an even more attractive proposition. Firstly, and most important, doing it yourself gives you, the author, total control over the life-span of the print run and also where it's being sold.

An alarming *Daily Telegraph* report revealed that some literary masterpieces have difficulty in selling 1000 copies; Booker prize-winners are on special offer in the book clubs before they are available on general release and an author is lucky if he sees 25p per hard-back book, instead of the usual £1 from retail outlets.

Adding to the general despondency, *The Author* reported that the sale of 6000 copies to a book club could result in an author's commission cheque 'so minuscule that something must surely have gone awry'. Not so. Although the author has spent years writing a book, he comes at the end of a long chain of costs and administration when it comes to profit sharing. With the abolition of the Net Book Agreement, author's profits via the publishing giants could sink even lower.

As we have seen, it is not unknown for books to be 'pulped' within weeks of publication date if the publishing house has got its marketing programme wrong, and unless provision has been made in the contract, the author's precious novel/non-fiction can disappear into a large, legal black hole. These horror stories are heard more and more frequently, so it is therefore doubly important to ensure that *before* signing on the dotted line, you retain all rights to your book after it goes out of print, is remaindered, or pulped.

Self-publishing, of course, runs as many risks, but I considered the length of time I wanted the reference book to remain in circulation (indefinitely), and the cost of re-printing (the same amount). Even if it took 2/3 years to sell 1000 copies, I should have recouped my costs after the first 200 sales at full price; taking bookseller's discount into account, I would need to sell approximately 400 copies to break even.

Payment & Costings:

There's more to evaluating your costings than getting a quote from a printer: *every service you require over and above printing is going to cost you extra.* With proof-reading costing around £7.00 per hour, a 200 page book could total more in proof-reading charges than it costs to have the text printed! Decide in advance whether your price includes postage and packing because these work out to approximately £1 per average size paperback book.

You also need to know in advance what your printer's payment terms are. When the *Malleus* went into production, I paid 50% as a deposit and the remainder when the books were ready for delivery. A sample copy was sent through the post for approval when the final invoice was due for payment. This enabled me to check for printer's errors - too late for text changes at this stage - before sending off the cheque. Avoid the printing companies that demand full payment up front; you have no redress if they've ruined your book or the work isn't up to standard.

Remember that if you sell through bookshops, you will be reducing your profit margin quite considerably while raising your blood pressure. If a bookseller is willing keep several copies in stock, he will expect a discount of 35-40%; single book sales through the trade would still expect 25%. Many bookstores work on anything up to 60-90 days credit and it is often necessary to send three or more statements before payment is made. Often they will insist on taking the book 'sale or return' and if they don't sell, you will land up with a pile of shop-soiled merchandise - state on your original invoice that returns are not acceptable without prior written agreement.

Author-Publisher Enterprise:

Just because you've decided to go it alone, it doesn't mean that there's no-one around when you want information, advice or assistance. All the services used to produce the *Malleus* came from the APN Directory and this meant there was a certain amount of confidence on both sides from the beginning.

As Trevor Lockwood explained: "Author-Publisher Network is more than an association for self-published writers. As an association of writers who publish their own material we are creating considerable interest. There are several reasons for this, not least the difficulty of finding a commercial publisher willing to accept work.

Publishing your own work is getting easier, all the experts you will require can be employed. Self-publishing does not mean you have to do everything - hire an expert, and all their acquired skill and wisdom for a short time. There are editors, proofreaders, short-run printers and some distributors who cater specifically for the author producing work that will have a limited audience.

Biographies abound, but no-one is interested except family and friends. Local history clearly has a limited appeal and together with poetry and first novels are best produced in small quantities, in the first instance. If sales are beyond wildest expectations there will be no difficulty in persuading a trade publisher to republish the work, or in producing another edition yourself. Starting small also means that all the mistakes can be removed at the reprint stage.

Everyone seems to be aware of the financial dangers of using a vanity publisher to help publish work. Yet we receive letters every day from writers who have parted with many thousands of pounds, and gained little more than a large invoice and a pile of books in the spare bedroom. Further, we see the same individuals liquidating one vanity publishing company, only to start up again in another name, leaving many unfortunates without books or cash. Nobody needs a vanity publisher.

"Why publish at all?" It is an important question that every writer must ask themselves. It certainly massages our egos and gives a measure of immortality, we all have something to say, and why not? Publishing your own work allows control and ensures the work will remain available, for as long as the writer wants it accessible in the public domain. Finally, if the work is successful, it will bring significantly greater financial return to its creator, who will retain the author's royalty, together with the publisher's profit."

What Are The Pitfalls?

Firstly, not realising the implications of allowing personal taste to transcend good marketing strategy can result in slower sales. My choice of cover was a fabulous reproduction of a medieval woodcut and it reflected *my* choice in art work. Nevertheless this was a wrong choice from a marketing point of view. Since the book is on the subject of witchcraft and aimed at the general reader, a garish image of devilry or a flaming pentagram might have more 'browser - appeal'. Although my cover is by far the more tasteful, it gives the book an appearance of being too high-brow and academic, according to those in the know.

Secondly, although I wish the book to remain in print for several years, I produced too many for a first run. Because new information was being made public after a government enquiry, it was important that the book be released around the same time. This resulted in too many 'typos' and, of course, the new information could not be included. Were I to produce a similar book now, I would have 1000 covers printed (this cuts down on re-run costs and gives spare covers for promotional purposes) and an initial print-run of 300. This would allow for corrections to be made for the second print-run and additional material included to keep the reference book up-to-date either by slotting into the text or as an appendix.

Thirdly, the most costly exercise was wasting too many books by sending them off to reviewers at national magazines and newspapers. Every 'freebie' eats into the self-publisher's profit and you are far better served by sending promotional material printed on the reverse side of your spare covers. If it sparks off an interest, they'll ask for it; if not, you've only wasted a single sheet of printed card. National reviewers rarely pay attention to self-published books - we can speculate on the reasons behind this but it merely wastes valuable copies to serve no purpose.

Quartos has received a large number of self-published novels and non-fiction for review over the years, and another fact that needs to be faced is that more often than not, the quality of the writing leaves a lot to be desired. Enthusiasm is no substitute for learning the Craft of writing and too many writers rush into self-publishing without finding their way around the market- place.

Lewis Hosegood:

"What were the pitfalls? The chief was the unexpectedly sheer hard labour in foot-slogging the finished product around the various points of sale, i.e. bookshops. Also the difficulty in getting money from them, having taken and sold copies. One well-known bookshop still owes me two years later despite having had invoices. What, with hindsight, would I do differently? Difficult to say short of taking on an accountant - my wife did most of the book-keeping, telephoning and correspondence."

Iris Bryce:

"It is very hard work going round the bookshops to sell personally and I still find it embarrassing to sell myself as it were. However, you'll certainly be surprised at the welcome you get from the larger booksellers, i.e. Smiths, Hammicks, etc. Many of their managers have said how they enjoy dealing personally with an author and no matter how small your business, they do seem to find time to talk to you - and very often buy.

I am now known in many Smith's shops and this is certainly due to my self-publishing activities. Fortunately it has helped enormously with my new book *Remembering Greenwich* because I must admit that I'm a little disappointed that it did not get taken up by the media. Although it was a National Award winning book and had a whole page publicity story of the award in *The Guardian*, this did not create any interest in the nationals when the book was published. Not one national paper, radio station or even local TV station took it up."

Would you do it again?

Despite the costly lessons learned in producing the *Malleus*, it made it much easier to decide to do it again with *From An Editor's Desk* although, with the benefit of hindsight, I went for a much shorter print run. For technical reasons we used a different company (Intype, Woodman Works, Durnsford Road, Wimbledon SW19 8DR) who suggested that we produce 500 copies of the cover and go for the shorter run of 250, since the cover is more cost effective to produce with our own local printer.

Even though there is the strong marketing potential through *Quartos*, writers' workshops and other outlets, this type of how-to book has a very short shelf life and will quickly become dated. Even if we don't go for a second print-run, the extra covers can be used as marketing leaflets to promote the book instead of sending review copies.

Lewis Hosegood:

"Is it a viable proposition? Depends on the product. Mine were both fiction - the first a collection of short stories, the second a mainstream novel. Neither sold well. But a friend who wrote and self-published a story of local interest (set around Corfe Castle in the 17th century) did extremely well with the National Trust as sponsor. Many bookshops ask the question: Is it of local interest? If so, you stand a much better chance. Non-fiction also does better. Surprisingly, perhaps poetry stands quite a good chance - probably because it's a smaller, cheaper booklet and people are prepared to fork out a few pounds. Would I do it again? The answer is probably no."

Iris Bryce:
"It was much harder to sell my children's book. I was lucky in that my price was very favourable when compared to most other books of the same size, and this was commented on by most book managers. However, I have only recovered about half of my outlay and although I still sell one or two at the odd lecture, I feel it will be sometime before I see much space under my stairs!

Thankfully I had sold out of my reprint and although I am being asked to reprint Canal book number two and possibly book 3, I've decided against it. I'd love a publisher to come along and ask for them but don't have much hope. However, if you really feel that you have written something that you are sure will be of interest to the general public then I would say go ahead and have a go at self-publishing."

Specialist short-run print companies like Antony Rowe and Intype will advise an author to go for the shortest cost-effective run on novels because they would rather have a satisfied customer than one bogged down with hundreds of unwanted books that no one wants to buy. (Remember that the author usually makes about 25p in royalties on a paperback book from a publisher, so if you aim for £1 on each sale, you could still be in profit if you've got your costings right.)

Intype have one regular client who produces 100 copies of every novel he's written to use as promotional material; even if they're not taken up by the mainstream publishing houses, he at least has the satisfaction of knowing that his books are being read in the local libraries. And who knows who else will read it ...

Electronic Publishing:

In Chapter One I suggested that writers should seriously consider the prospect of increasing technology making it a necessity for them to develop computer skills if they wish to keep abreast of 21st century publishing. We have now come full circle. The serious writer must always have an eye to the future and before too long there will be a further option - electronic publishing. As Trevor Lockwood of APN pointed out:

"With Internet, an international network of computers, it is now becoming easier to publish your own book - electronically. No publishers. No printers. Your word-processed text is converted into a book format that is read from the screen. There may be few customers at present but that will change. As writers we must become aware of these changes. The structures we have found so acceptable to contain the written word for so many years are changing. The novel, short story and poem printed on paper and bound into a book will remain for sufficient years to keep may of us content. Yet today's children have a different perception of the world ... They will accept that the electronic transfer is easier, more efficient and ecologically acceptable."

And we're not talking out of our own small sphere of publishing interests. I am currently investigating the possibilities and pitfalls of advertising the *Malleus* on the Internet - so far, in under three weeks there have been 40 enquiries for further details. *Quartos* has already gone on to it for a test-run and received enquiries for details of the Open Writing Competition from overseas as a result. Moe Sherrard-Smith has written a computer programme version of *The Essential Guide To Novel Writing*.

Moe Sherrard-Smith:

"Writing material for a programme was something very enjoyable but entirely new for me; but as so many writers use computers and are used to speedy access to information via the screen, it seemed a logical progression from my co-authored book, *Write A Successful Novel*. Beginners have to remember that novels don't just happen, they are created. The Guide intends to foster the creative process.

The programme is available on Amstrad PCW disc, with a PC version due shortly. *The Guide* takes writers through all the stages of a book, from initial idea to submitting the completed manuscripts to agents or publishers. A special data-base has scores of alphabetically arranged topics to access, together with some questions and model answers on subjects including aspects of characterisation and viewpoints, and submission letters. As a bonus guide, *Making Sense of Essay Writing* by former University lecturer Rex Last has also been adapted for disk."

At the time of going to print, Peter James's novel *Host*, published by Penguin had become the world's first electronic mainstream novel, containing the same text as the hardback and paperback versions and produced on floppy disk. This year *Host* is being published on the Internet and anyone with access will be able to read it free. According to an article in *The Electronic Author*, the author considers it to be a 'hugely interesting experiment' since there's the possibility of a large number of the 30 million+ Internet users wanting to buy it.

Doesn't he have any fears about pirate copies being made? Apparently it's very expensive to download a complete book - "The telephone bill mounts up while you are logged on and the paper for a print out, plus the cost of toner cartridges, would put the cost of doing so at upwards of £50. Cheaper to go out and buy it!" he says.

However, as I've said before, all this does not mean that mainstream publishers will, or should, be ignored when it comes to publishing full-length books. We all have dreams of writing a best-seller and without the 'big names' in publishing we don't stand a chance of reaching out for that dream. If your book has been turned down by a dozen agents and publishers, try to view it objectively. Self-publication isn't the complete answer but what it does give is the opportunity to shape our own destiny as a published writer rather than having to sit back and wait for Lady Luck to come calling.

Recommended Reading:

An invaluable guide to any form of self-publishing, *Marketing For Small Publishers* by Godber, Webb and Smith (journeyman) offers a practical, step-by-step guide to planning a marketing programme, promotional mailings and direct sales, dealing with the media, selling books to bookshops and wholesalers, and researching libraries and specialist markets. ISBN: 1-85172-035-9

How To Publish A Book by Robert Spicer (How To Books) de-mystifies the process of self-publishing in practical business-like steps. From developing the initial idea, to legal and commercial considerations, deciding the right price and print run, handling typesetters, print and other suppliers, designing the cover, through to essential practicalities such as storage, packing, direct sales, invoicing, using book representatives, organising publicity and much more. It also discusses the main pitfalls to avoid and is full of realistic guidance on how to achieve your objectives at a profit. ISBN 1-85703-071-0

How To Publish Yourself by Peter Finch (Alison & Busby) shows that publishing your own work can be both rewarding and enjoyable. His extremely practical guide to going it alone, based largely on his own experiences, covers every aspect of the enterprise from start to finish. ISBN: 0-85031-777-0

Tailpiece:

Having read through the first draft of *From An Editor's Desk,* a journalist friend commented: "It's a depressing little book, but I wish there'd been something like it around when I first started writing. It tells the truth, unpalatable as it is, that writing is not easy and that selling it is even more difficult."

Unlike many how-to books on creative writing, the information contained in *From An Editor's Desk* is not confined to the opinions of one author/tutor/journalist; in an attempt to show an overall picture, I have invited as many differing viewpoints as possible. Some endorse, others contradict, but all are valid comments from experienced authors and freelance writers. Where necessary, various points have been repeated for maximum effect.

The current market place remains extremely limiting for fiction writers, giving those willing to tackle non-fiction and poetry the slight advantage in the publication stakes. Agreed, commercialism *does* place strictures on individual writing styles but producing material for a specific target market provides a valuable exercise in understanding editorial and publishing requirements of those who are in a position to buy!

All this advice on producing 'popular' articles and fiction, however, does not mean you should refrain from working on the novel or short stories *you want to write* - it can be undertaken in tandem with your commercial output and can even gain from it. Remember, market demands are fickle and what is highly unprofitable fiction today could become tomorrow's best seller.

The publishing world is never going to return to the 'good old days' but attitudes are starting to change. According to an article in *The Daily Telegraph* (August 1995), small independent publishing houses are beginning to re-appear in the belief that the monopoly of the big conglomerates - 'the Seven Sisters, as they are known in the trade' - are over. Books by new authors *may* stand a better chance with the smaller houses but where will publishing go from there?

With the collapse of the Net Book Agreement, there are fears that the smaller, independent publishers who often discover and promote new writers will be seriously under threat. According to Malcolm Bradbury, writing in *The Daily Telegraph*, "... the writer, once the independent, radical, thinking agent of the free imagination, must now learn to compete with the cabbages and (Stephen) Kings in the supermarket or bookstore."

Perhaps more and more authors will consider publishing and marketing their own books. In the Spring 1995 issue of *The Author* (The Society of Authors), an article posed eight essential questions to ask before you even think about publishing yourself. By June 1995, Christopher Sinclair-Stevenson, an earlier casualty of independent publishing, wrote in *The Times* that would-be authors might do best to take the DIY route to publishing their work, since the problems involved cannot be worse than dealing with publishers. The September 1995 issue of *Country Living* included a full-length feature article on the self-publishing careers of five 'real' authors who have decided to go it alone.

Whatever your road to publication, understanding your own individual interests and keeping up-to-date with changes in the mercurial world of publishing is an essential part of the craft for the would-be *serious* writer. Commit to memory those three key-words essential to any professional author, features writer, story-teller or poet:

information - discipline - originality

because ignoring them will only lead to continual disappointment.

There's no short cut to publication, no easy road to success. Writing for publication is about knowing the market-place, so realise and accept right from the start, that *no-one can be taught to be a writer* - you can only successfully develop the techniques of the craft and build on the ability you already possess.

See you in print!

Suzanne Ruthven

Useful Contacts:

Acclaim Magazine: The New Writers' Club, P O Box 101, Tunbridge Wells, Kent TN4 8YD.

Allison & Busby Ltd: 5 The Lodge, Richmond Way, London W12 8LW.

Arvon Foundation: Totleigh Barton. Sheepwash, Beaworthy, Devon EX21 5NS; also at Lumb Bank, Heptonsall, Hebden Bridge, West Yorkshire HX7 6DF and a pilot scheme at Moniack Mhor, Moniack, Kirkhall, Inverness IV5 7PQ

Association of Little Presses: 30 Greenhill, Hampstead High Street, London NW3 5UA

Author-Publisher Network: 12 Mercers, Hawkhurst, Kent TN18 4LH.

A&C Black Publishers: P O Box 19, Huntingdon, Cambs PE19 3SF.

Book & Magazine Collector: 45 St Mary's Road, London W5 5RQ

British Amateur Press Association: Michaelmas, Cimarron Close, South Woodham Ferrers, Essex CM3 5PB.

The Comedy Writers Association: 61 Parry Road, Ashmore Park, Wolverhapton WV11 2PS

Envoi Magazine: 44 Rudyard Road, Biddulph Moor, Stoke on Trent, Staffs ST8 7JN

FLAIR Network: 5 Delavall Walk, Eastbourne BN23 6ER

Freelance Market News: Cumberland House, Lissadell Street, Salford, Manchester M6 6GG

The Gothic Society: Chatham House, Gosshill House, Chislehurst, Kent BR7 5NS

How-To Books: Plymbridge House, Estover Road, Plymouth PL6 7PZ.

Metropolitan: 19 Victoria Avenue, Didsbury, Manchester M20 2GY

New Playwrights Trust: Interchange Studios, 15 Dalby Street, London NW5 3NQ

New Writer's Club (see Acclaim Magazine):

Oriel Bookshop: The Friary, Cardiff CF1 9BU

Piatkus (Publishers) Ltd: 5 Windmill Street, London W1P 1HF

The Poetry Library: South Bank Centre, Royal Festival Hall, (Level 5, Red Side) London SE1 8XX

Quartos Magazine: BCM-Writer, London WC1N 3XX

Real Writers: P O Box 170, Chesterfield. Derbyshire S40 1FE
Rialto Magazine: 32 Grosvenor Road, Norwich, Norfolk NR2 2PZ
The Romantic Novelists' Association: 35 Ruddlesway, Windsor SL4 5SF
Scriptease Editorial: Finchden, Sandhurst, Cranbrook, Kent TN18 5JS
Society of Civil Service Authors: 8 Bawtree Close, Sutton, Surrey
The Society of Authors: 84 Drayton Gardens, London SW10 9SD
The Society of Women Writers & Journalists: 110 Whitehall Road,
London E4 6DW
Southampton Writers' Conference: The Conference Organiser,
University of Southampton, Southampton SO9 5NH.
Staple Magazine: Tor Cottage, 81 Cavendish Road. Matlock, Derbys
DE4 3HD
The Taliesin Trust - Ty Newydd: Llanysturndwy, Cricieth, Gwynedd
LL52 0LW
Tees Valley Writer: 57 The Avenue, Linthorpe, Middlesborough,
Cleveland TS5 6QU
University of the Third Age (Writers' Network): National Office,
1 Stockwell Street, London SW9 9JF.
The Welsh Academy: 3rd Floor, Mount Stuart House, Mount Stuart
Square, Cardiff CF1 6DQ
The Writer's Advice Centre: Adam Cottage, St. Mary's Street, Axbridge,
Somerset BS26 2BN
Writers' Monthly: 29 Turnpike Lane, London N8 0EP
Writer's News: P O Box 4, Nairn IV12 4HU
Zene: 5 Martin's Lane, Witcham, Ely. Cambs CB6 2LB

Index